PS
214
V4   Vedder,
1972   American writers of to-day.

JUL   2000

Date Due

		JUN 2004
		JUL 03
		JUL X X 2015

AMERICAN

WRITERS OF TO-DAY

BY

HENRY C. VEDDER

*A perfect Judge will read each work of Wit
With the same spirit that its author writ:
Survey the Whole, nor seek slight faults to find
Where nature moves, and rapture warms the mind.*
                    POPE: Essay on Criticism.

Essay Index Reprint Series

BOOKS FOR LIBRARIES PRESS
FREEPORT, NEW YORK

74-1756

First Published 1894
Reprinted 1972

Library of Congress Cataloging in Publication Data

Vedder, Henry Clay, 1853-1935.
    American writers of to-day.

    (Essay index reprint series)
    Reprint of the 1894 ed.
    CONTENTS: Edmund Clarence Stedman.--Francis Parkman.--
William Dean Howells. [etc.]
    1. American literature--19th century--Bio-biblio-
graphy. I. Title.
PS214.V4 1972   .810'.9'004   72-8513
ISBN 0-8369-7334-8

PRINTED IN THE UNITED STATES OF AMERICA

TO HER

WHOSE SYMPATHETIC COMPANIONSHIP,

WHOSE LOVE OF THE GOOD,

THE BEAUTIFUL,

THE TRUE,

HAVE BEEN AN INSPIRATION IN ALL MY WORK

THROUGH MANY HAPPY YEARS,

I DEDICATE

THIS BOOK.

PREFACE.

JOHN QUINCY ADAMS once defined luncheon as "a reflection on breakfast and an insult to dinner." In a similar spirit, one might define a preface as a reflection on the author's skill and an insult to his readers' intelligence; for, if a book requires elaborate exegesis, if its purpose demands careful explanation, something must needs be wrong with either book or reader. Nobody need feel under the slightest obligation, therefore, to read this preface; but should it occur to some one to glance a second time at this page, let him be assured that these studies of contemporary American literature make no pretence of being complete, comprehensive, exhaustive. There was a vague purpose in the author's mind, when he began writing, to supplement these chapters with some attempt at a general survey of the American literature of our own time, after the manner of Mrs. Oliphant's "Victorian Age of English Literature." This would have given them more formal completeness, even if it did not otherwise add to their value. Should the reception of his

book encourage him to persevere, he may yet fulfil
that intention.

In the meantime, he ventures to hope that what
he has done may fill a vacant place.   There is very
little that makes any pretence of being serious criticism of the writers of our own day.   Let any one
ransack even a large library, and he will in most
cases go away empty-handed of books that will aid
him in the study and comprehension of current literature.   Some of our leading periodicals contain
reviews of lately published books that are worthy
to rank with the best critical writing; but these
reviews only partially supply the reader's wants.
What he desires is an intelligent and critical account
of an author's whole performance, not a review of
any particular work; something that will help him
to comprehend the nature and value of a writer's
contribution to our literature, to estimate his significance, to perceive his characteristics and idiosyn-
cracies, — in a word, to read him understandingly.
If these studies have any value, it is their fitness in
some sort to satisfy this desire.   The writer does
not affect what Scott felicitously called " the big
bow-wow style," nor has he any ambition to be a
Jeffrey with a " This will never do " for anything that
he does not himself like; still less does he aspire
to make and unmake authors' reputations.   The
motto placed on the titlepage has been throughout
borne in mind.   He has tried to read our American

authors sympathetically, intelligently, diligently, and to report as well as he is able the results of this reading. Making no claims to infallibility, he has striven to give his report honestly, and

> "nothing extenuate
> Nor set down aught in malice."

Partly for the convenience of those who lack other books of reference, partly because the facts recited throw a side-light on the literary work of the writers studied, some biographical details are interwoven with the critical remarks. If to any the book seem to lose dignity because of this, possibly in the judgment of other readers this feature will add to its interest and value.

New York, October 2, 1894.

CONTENTS.

AMERICAN WRITERS OF TO-DAY.

I.

EDMUND CLARENCE STEDMAN.

AMERICA has as yet produced no poet who was poet and nothing else. No counterpart of a Wordsworth or a Tennyson, conscious of his high calling, has devoted his life to the faithful and single-hearted worship of the Muses. This may be, in part, due to the hard conditions of life in a new world. Every man has had to face the problem of making a living, and we are even now only beginning to see grow up among us a leisure class. A people that have had to subdue the wilderness, to tunnel the mountains, to bridge rivers, to build railways and telegraphs and factories, to dig wealth out of the bowels of the earth, may be pardoned if they have somewhat neglected the worship of the beautiful in eager quest of the useful. Our country has thus far been too deeply intent on utilitarian aims, its ideals have been too gross and unspiritual, for the up-bringing of great poets.

For, even had the poet been born, he had been given scant encouragement to devote his life to his art. A Tennyson, a Scott, a Byron, receives princely sums for his verse, but what American poet has been able to live by his art alone? Of all our

Scant rewards
of American
poesy
singers, Longfellow came nearest to this, yet he was far past middle life before he was able to surrender his bread-winning profession and give all his time to literature. Only one born to affluence, like a Browning, can venture to devote his life to work for which his fellows show so slight esteem and offer a reward so niggard.

As a compensation, in some sort, for the lack of great poets, America has been dowered with an unusual proportion of clever men of letters, — poets, but not poets solely; men whose Yankee shrewdness and adaptability have enabled them to do many kinds of work, and to touch nothing that they have not adorned. Poe, Bryant, Longfellow, Emerson, Lowell, Holmes, among the dead, Stedman, Aldrich, Howells, among the living, are names that at once suggest themselves to us. It may well be that our literature as a whole is more brilliant and many-sided than it would have been had these and others been able to give themselves wholly to poetry. There are those who hold that, if one has the true afflatus in any degree, and is conscious of a message to deliver to the world, he will find a way and a time to speak it forth. Much may plausibly be said for this view of the case; one instinctively disbelieves in the " mute, inglorious Miltons," for had they been Miltons they had been neither mute nor inglorious. And yet, there may easily be such a thing as the partial delivery of a message. The skylark will surely sing, but we may believe that he will soar higher and pipe a clearer, more melodious note, when the heavens are propitious.

I.

EDMUND CLARENCE STEDMAN was born at Hartford, Conn., October 8, 1833. He is a scion of the purest New England stock. Like many other men of genius, he seems to have inherited his mental and moral traits largely from his mother, a sister of William E. Dodge, and daughter of the Rev. Aaron Cleveland, great-grandfather of Grover Cleveland. Quite early in life he showed special aptitude for lit- An early aptitude for literature, and gave promise of at least con- ture. siderable talent. While a student at Yale College he won honors in Greek and English, obtaining first prize with a poem on "Westminster Abbey" that was published in the " Yale Literary Miscellany" in 1851, For some boyish escapade he was suspended from college in his junior year, and never returned to take his degree. What his offence was does not appear, but that it was no serious affair is evidenced by the mildness of the penalty, and still more by the subsequent action of his college, which in 1871 restored him to his class rank and conferred on him the degree of Master of Arts.

His college course being terminated in this summary way, young Stedman adopted journalism as his calling, and, after a brief and not too profitable experience with country newspapers in Connecticut, he found a place on the staff of the " New York Tribune " in 1854. Here he remained until 1860, when he joined the staff of the " New York World," and for some time served as war correspondent. As a journalist, one gathers that he was faithful, hard-working, and reasonably successful, without being brilliant. Perhaps enough of his strict New England training still abode with him to hinder his advancement. One requires an ample stock of native assurance and an acquired hardihood above common, and must overboard with all his fine scruples and nice sensitiveness of conscience, if he A trial of jour- would get to the top in journalism. It may nalism. be reasonably conjectured that the discovery of this had something to do with Mr. Stedman's course ; if so, it is to his credit that he was not willing to pay the price of success in the calling he had ignorantly chosen. Another reason doubtless actuated him ; he still cherished dreams of becoming a poet. He had continued to woo the Muses at intervals, with a flattering degree of success ; and he had grounds for hoping that, with added years and experience, if he could attain pecuniary independence, he might write his name high on the roll of American singers.

After a brief experience of office-holding, under Attorney-General Bates, Mr. Stedman returned to New York, and in 1864 became a stock-broker. Those were times in which fortunes were daily made " on the street," and the still youthful broker may have cherished visions of a speedy retirement, and the spending of the best years of his life among his books, in the practice of his beloved art. If such A plunge into Wall Street. were his day-dreams, this modern Alnaschar soon found them rudely shattered. He was not long in learning that if fortunes are quickly won in Wall Street, they are as quickly swept away again. It was another lake of Tantalus to the would-be poet. Several times he saw his fortune just within his grasp, and once it seemed to be fully attained, when a turn of fortune's wheel compelled him to begin over again. What seemed at the beginning to be but the occupation of a few years at most, turned out to be the grinding work of a lifetime. Within a few years, if rumor is to be trusted, dame Fortune has been more kind, but her favors have come too late. The productive years of stalwart manhood are gone. The desire of great achievement doubtless remains, but the full opportunity can never return. It is the old story: *Ah ! si la jeunesse savait — si la vieillesse pouvait !* "When I was a boy," says Thackeray somewhere, " I used to pass a confectioner's window. There was taffy in it; I wanted some, but the taffy was a shilling, and I had none. Now I have the shilling, but I don't care for taffy."

II.

MR. STEDMAN'S versifying began, as we have seen, in his college days. His prize poem he has never reprinted, possibly because he shares Macaulay's opinion that a prize poem is like a prize sheep, and that "prize sheep are good for nothing but to make tallow candles, and prize poems are good for nothing but to light them." It must be confessed that Tennyson's "Timbuctoo" is a powerful confirmation of this theory, and it might be difficult to name any other production that would tend to disprove it. But Mr. Stedman has not exercised this severity in the case of all his *juvenilia*, and for this one is grateful, since we are now able to trace the growth of his genius and his art as we could not otherwise. What among his early writings he deemed worthy of preservation, he included Poems, Lyric in "Poems, Lyric and Idyllic," which appeared in 1860 with the imprint of Charles Scribner. The verses that formed this volume may still be found in the author's collected works, of which they fill the first eighty-five pages.

This was a rather remarkable book for a young man of twenty-seven to print, — remarkable chiefly for its promise, as was but natural, but remarkable in some measure for actual achievement also. The verse manifested present as well as potential power. We find, what we might expect, obvious traces of the influence of other poets, the result of generous admiration and unconscious imitation. There is more than a suggestion of Hood and Saxe, especially of the latter, in "The Diamond Wedding;" and one asks himself whether "Penelope" would have been written except by a poet who had read and even studied Tennyson's "Ulysses." "Flood Tide," too, is in the spirit, as well as the measure, of "Locksley Hall," and couplets like

the following might well have been among the fragments that the elder poet was unable to work into his
theme: —

" Shame upon all listless dreamers early hiding from the strife,
Sated with some little gleaning of the harvest-fields of life ! "

" Calm, and slowly lifting upward, rose the eastern glory higher,
Gilding sea, and shore, and vessel, and the city-crowning spire."

In " The Sleigh-Ride," again, we have a reminiscence
of Shelley, and a little scrutiny would doubtless detect
other cases of similarity.   Fortunate is the youthful
poet who chooses such masters as these in his art.
But there are verses here in which the poet utters a
note of his own; " The Singer " is a nearly perfect bit
of workmanship, and " The Freshet " is an idyll that
only country-bred readers can fully appreciate.

Probably the most spirited piece in the book was,
" How Old Brown Took Harper's Ferry," and it still
ranks among the best poems inspired by   The John
the event that it commemorates; indeed,   Brown ballad.
one is much inclined to rank it above all competitors.
Though the poet skips the hard places in Brown's
Kansas career, — if he knew of the Pottawotamie mas-
sacres when he wrote, — he indulges in less unmeasured
hero-worship than has been the fashion in certain circles of the North.   But if his poem would hardly have
passed muster then (and it would still less pass now)
as a cool historic estimate of John Brown, it is still
worthy of respect as an outburst of lofty moral sentiment and passionate patriotic feeling, however ill-

chosen the occasion, or unworthy the object. Almost
prophetic, in the light of subsequent events, seems this
closing stanza, written before Brown's execution, in
answer to the cry of " Hang him ! " that went up from
the South : —

" But, Virginians, don't do it ! for I tell you that the flagon,
    Filled with blood of Old Brown's offspring, was first poured
        by Southern hands ;
    And each drop from Old Brown's life-veins, like the red gore
        of the dragon,
    May spring up a vengeful Fury, hissing through your slave-
        worn lands !
              And Old Brown,
              Ossawatomie Brown,
  May trouble you more than ever, when you 've nailed his coffin
    down ! "

The publication of this volume may have convinced
the judicious few that a poet had appeared who " knew
to sing and build the lofty rhyme," but it certainly
made no great sensation. On the whole, it may be
said to have been " favorably received," — a phrase
that has a pretty sound and is usefully vague. The
times were not auspicious for the launching of poetical ventures. The people of the North were too
intent on sterner themes to regard verses, except
such as had a martial ring or appealed to the rising
antislavery fervor. The John Brown ballad was the
only poem that was keyed to the feeling of the day,
and therefore the book had only *un succès d'estime*,
though it deserved more. All things considered, it
was fortunate to escape a worse fate.

III.

THE second period of Mr. Stedman's poetic activity is the decade between 1860 and 1870. It is distinguished by the publication of two volumes, — "Alice of Monmouth" (New York, 1864) and "The Blameless Prince" (Boston, 1869), — and was rounded off by the issue in 1873 of a complete edition of the poetical works, bearing the imprint of Ticknor and Fields. It was during this ten or twelve years that the greater part of Mr. Stedman's work as poet was done. Absorbed as he was, first by the most exacting and exhausting of callings, and afterwards by the hardly less distracting cares of business, he was quite unable to repress the spirit that strove within him for utterance in verse.

"Alice of Monmouth" was described in the subtitle as "An Idyll of the Great War," and other poems were included in the volume. This title-poem was a romance in verse. Experiments of this kind have been sometimes phenomenally successful, but not always. Scott gained an unbounded popularity, as permanent as it was sudden, by means of An Idyll of the Great War. his "Marmion" and "The Lady of the Lake," but even he failed disastrously in some of his later ventures. Tennyson, a far greater poet, though he measurably succeeded in "The Princess," failed dismally in "Maud," which is only saved from oblivion by two, or at most three, exquisite lyrics embedded in the rubbish. The younger Lytton, as "Owen

Meredith," achieved immediate but transitory fame among sentimental misses with " Lucile," — thanks to heroic stealing from George Sand, — but it is now pretty well agreed that while " Lucile " may be a romance, it is not a poem. " Alice of Monmouth " was neither a disastrous failure nor a marvellous success. It is a story that ought to have appealed to American readers, in the midst of the Civil War, with peculiar force. It has poetic merit of a high order, but it never became a popular book. This fate is not a little hard to justify, or even to understand. There was no lack of popular interest in the theme; readers greedily devoured, as fast as the groaning presses could turn them out, war novels of the most trashy and sensational kind, written in an indescribable style, that can be pronounced neither English nor American; there seemed to be literally no limit to the appetite of the public for reading of this kind. It may be that the workmanship of this poem was too fine, its passion too sublimated, its charm too ethereal, to please the multitude. It is still so unfamiliar to American readers, of more than ordinary intelligence and culture, that one might quote from it almost anywhere and vainly challenge a roomful of such people to identify the passage. One exception should be noted, — which, however, is only partially an exception, — and that is the spirited " Cavalry Song," which is the fifth number of Part XI. of the poem: —

> " Our good steeds snuff the evening air,
>   Our pulses with their purpose tingle;

> The foeman's fires are twinkling there;
>   He leaps to hear our sabres jingle!
>   HALT!
>   Each carbine sends its whizzing ball:
>   Now, cling! clang! forward all,
>   Into the fight! "

This song of three stanzas is, as it deserves to be, one of the best known and most admired of Stedman's poems. Yet it is safe to say, not one in a thousand of those who have read it in some anthology of American verse holds it for anything but an independent lyric, or would fail to be astonished on hearing that it is but a small portion of a poem of some fifty closely printed octavo pages.

"The Blameless Prince" is even less known. In this case one cannot wish the verdict of the public reversed. It is not a wholesome poem. A vein of cynicism runs through it that quite vitiates it for those who still believe that men are true and women chaste. The burden of the story is that those who are praised by the world for purity and honor are sinners in secret; and yet, being such sinners, deserve that we should pity and spare them, for

> " He who brightest is, and best,
>   Still may fear the secret test
>   That shall try his heart aright."

A tale whose moral is so immoral is deservedly neglected by readers. It is the one thing in all Mr. Stedman's writings, whether verse or prose, that is not clean and bracing.

In the collected poems of 1873 were most of those with which Mr. Stedman's name is most closely connected, — those of which one instinctively thinks whenever his name is mentioned. There were four spirited war-lyrics — " Sumter," " Wanted — a Man," " Gettysburg," and " Kearney at Seven Pines " — which, of their kind, are scarcely surpassed in our literature. All of these but the " Sumter" have been included, along with the " Cavalry Song," in the collection of " American War Ballads and Lyrics " made by Mr. George Cary Eggleston; and every reader of taste will pronounce them to be among the very best things in the two volumes. Very few of the great mass of poems called forth by the Civil War still stir the blood like these.

The first " complete " edition.

Verses of a more peaceful sort were also first gathered in this volume. " Pan in Wall Street " is deservedly a prime favorite with everybody who can appreciate a blend of fancy and humor. Who has not felt the charm of " Laura, My Darling," the poem *par excellence* of all wedded lovers? What reminiscences of boyhood days and rural sports in " Country Sleighing" and "The Doorstep," — the latter worthy to live alongside of " Zekle's Courtin'." And where is there a prettier child's poem than " What the Winds Bring"?

In all these later poems there is but one that even suggests the manner of any other poet. One may be wrong about that instance, but in the " Dartmouth Ode" are tones that seem like echoes of Lowell's " Commemoration Ode." The resemblance is more in the structure of the verse and the general manner than in anything more specific, except in one case to be noted. Of any actual imitation there is of course no trace; there are no verbal similarities; there is not even the same manner of handling the theme; and the theme itself is distinct from that of Lowell's ode, though similar. Still, the eighth strophe, in which the character of Chase is described and eulogized, impresses one as strikingly like Lowell's familiar tribute to Lincoln. The impression is so spontaneous and so strong, one can hardly resist an inference that Lowell's ode suggested in some degree Mr. Stedman's, and in particular that the two passages specified are thus related. One hesitates about saying this, but as the resemblance is no closer than Mr. Stedman has himself traced between Tennyson and Theocritus, it can do no harm to let it stand. It is certainly no worse to owe a hint to a contemporary poet than to one who has been dead long enough to be forgotten, though perhaps the choice is less prudent.

Mr. Stedman's latest verse has shown no falling-off from that of his prime. He had not passed his prime, indeed, when his last book appeared, — "Hawthorne and Other Poems" (Boston, 1876). These verses were included in the "Household Edition" of his poetical works (Boston, 1884). On various occasions, unfornately too infrequent, he has broken silence since that time, but he has published no volume. His careful There is, in this latest verse, the same workmanship. careful and conscientious literary art, the same high purpose, that mark all his best work. None of our American poets has been less content with "the first fine careless rapture" of song, none has spared less the labor of the file. Not that his poems appear labored, that they smell of the lamp — that were indeed crude literary art; rather his verse by its very perfectness of form, its apparently unstudied simplicity and easy grace, gives token of the severe labor without which this supreme excellence is unattainable.

IV.

WITH the interruption of his original work, began Mr. Stedman's labors as a critic. A sort of introduction to this was the editing, in conjunction with Mr. T. B. Aldrich, of "Cameos from Landor" (Boston, 1874). His actual critical work, however, was not undertaken until the following year, when the first of what proved to be an extended series of essays was Victorian Poets and Poets of America. published in "Scribner's Magazine" (now "The Century"). One series of these essays was collected into a volume, with the title "Victorian Poets" (Boston, 1875, London, 1876); another and later collection being entitled "Poets of America" (Boston, 1886). The popularity of both volumes was immediate, great, and well deserved; the former has reached its twenty-first edition, while the latter is in its eleventh. Nor is the reason of this popularity far to seek. For the service undertaken in these essays but one other American could be thought of as the author's equal in equipment;

and while to Lowell we may concede equal or superior
learning and breadth of vision, and a style quite unapproachable, we cannot grant that in equipoise, in
impartial judgment, in coolness of mind, he was Mr.
Stedman's equal. Lowell, had he attempted a similar
task, would have written delightful essays, in themselves contributions of high value to our literature,
apart from their critical content; but in saying this
does not one hint at their probable defect? They
would have been rather literature than criticism. In
our author's case, temperament, scholarship, and experience combined to make him almost the ideal
critic. While by no means incapable of generous
admiration, he is not prone to let the
warmth of his emotion obscure the clear- His equipment as a critic.
ness of his mental operations. His judgment is not
biassed by affection; he knows how to be kindly just,
but he does not know how to be weakly partial. The
partisan of no theory of art, the champion of no school,
a citizen of the world, his candid spirit and catholic
taste inspire confidence, not merely in the rectitude of
his intent, but in the trustworthiness of his interpreta-
tions, the correctness of his canons, and the accuracy
of his conclusions. The uninstructed reader instinct-
ively feels that he is following a safe guide; and, while
the instructed reader may differ from the critic on
questions of detail, he will differ seldom, and then
with modest self-distrust; and he is not likely to dispute the sincerity or sanity of that which he declines
to accept as authoritative.

Every man has the defects of his qualities, as the French say. Mr. Stedman is so thorough an artist in verse, he comprehends so fully the resources as well as the limitations of his art, that he lacks patience with one who seems careless of the mere form of expression. This makes his criticism of Browning unsatisfactory, because unsympathetic. All that he says is true, or at

His limitations. least ingenious, but one is conscious throughout the essay that the critic has failed to grasp and express the whole truth. Indeed, no man to whom poetry is primarily an art can understand Browning. Mr. Stedman fails, with the best intentions in the world, frankly and sincerely to admire Browning, and his attempt to force an admiration that he does not feel makes his criticism less valuable than is its wont. This is the more curious, because he so ardently admires Walt Whitman, — a man who was not only not an artist, but who lost no opportunity to tell the world how much he despised art.

One of Mr. Stedman's largest critical undertakings has been the editing, in connection with Miss Ellen

The Library of American Literature. M. Hutchinson, of a " Library of American Literature" (New York, 1888–1891). This library has filled ten large octavo volumes. The making of the selections, and the preparation of the large amount of critical and biographical matter accompanying them, gave abundant scope for the exercise of the largest learning, the soundest judgment, and the best taste. Regarding the value of his labors there is no difference of opinion. By common

consent this is the completest collection of representative writings of American authors, and the best guide
to a systematic study of our literature, that has ever
been made.

The latest claim of Mr. Stedman on our gratitude
is the publication of his lectures on " The Nature and
Elements of Poetry." In this volume he at once dis-
cusses the fundamental principles of the art of poetry
and illustrates them from the practice of the great
masters of the art. The book is thus both creed and
criticism. He has little faith in untutored genius, in
those who compose by the light of nature The Nature and Elements of Poetry.
and pour forth in the ears of an astonished
world "their profuse strains of unpremeditated art."
To him poetry is not merely an art, but the noblest
of the arts, and not the least difficult, — as little to be
acquired without study and practice as likely to be
acquired by practice and study solely.

Definition of terms is always desirable and generally
indispensable; and a definition of poetry is none the
less helpful in a discussion of this kind because the
thing to be defined is vague and elusive, and refuses
to be adequately expressed in words. Mr. Stedman's
definition is broad and inclusive, yet sufficiently definite: " Poetry is rhythmical, imaginative language,
expressing the invention, taste, thought, passion, and
insight, of the human soul." It is the art of expression
in verse, in briefer terms. But this implies, first of all,
that the poet have some thought requiring imaginative
expression, and that he be capable of giving his

thought a fitting form. This is why he is poet (*poietes*, maker, creator), and without this he is a mere mechanical versifier. But how to have such a thought? This requires " the vision and the faculty divine," the power to see into the very heart of things, the creative insight — what, in a word, we mean by " genius." But thus far poetry is not sufficiently differentiated from prose; we need the further qualification that it is the *rhythmical* expression of the visions of genius. Even this does not completely differentiate poetry from prose, for there is a prose rhythm, and prose may be so imaginative, so like to poetry in all save form, as to be best described by the term " poetic prose." The rhythm of poetry is marked by regularity, while the characteristic of prose rhythm is flexibility and variety. Just as soon as sentences become rhythmical according to a fixed alternation of syllable and accent, in regular sequence, the form of expression is no longer prose but verse. Mr. Stedman's definition Poetry defined. should, therefore, be amended somewhat as follows: " Poetry is the expression in imaginative language and in regular rhythm, of the human soul's invention, taste, thought, passion, and insight."

That this element of regularity is the differentiating feature of verse, becomes evident when one examines the masters of prose. There is rhythmical, imaginative language in the prose of Milton, of Landor, of De Quincey, of Carlyle; but no two successive sentences have the same rhythm. In whole pages of Dickens and of Blackmore, on the other hand, one

finds that regularity of rhythm which is distinctive of
verse. Some of the most sonorous and majestic passages in English literature would be spoiled by the
change of a word here and there, in no way affecting
the sense, but utterly destroying the rhythm; while
the prose style of Dickens and Blackmore would be
happily mended by such changes as would break up
the regularity of their rhythmical passages.

Rhythmical regularity, however, is only one aspect
of the form of expression that we call poetry. Given
this, and the fundamental intuition of genius, poetry
becomes effective, according to Mr. Stedman, through
beauty, feeling, and imagination. Any work of art
that produces a serious and lasting impression will be
found in the end to owe its effect to beauty. That
which is merely bizarre and audacious can have no
enduring charm, and endurance is the test of worth in
art. Beauty in poetry is of two kinds: beauty of
construction and beauty of detail. Of the Beauty the
chief element
former, the chief element is simplicity, of poetry.
which must be attained through naturalness; while in
the case of the latter, richness and variety must be
carefully restrained from the vice of over decoration.
But, above all, poetry to be beautiful must have the
attribute that we can name yet cannot describe, —
charm.

A step further Mr. Stedman goes. Truth and
beauty, in the last reduction, he declares to be equivalent terms, and "beauty is the unveiled shining
countenance of truth," — a prose version of Keats's

> "Beauty is truth, truth beauty, — that is all
>   Ye know on earth, and all ye need to know."

It follows from this that a truth, to be beautiful, must be a whole truth. This principle excludes from poetry all didacticism, which is essentially the preach‑ ment of the gospel of half-truths by those who have not the insight to perceive the soul of truth, the expression of which is always beauty. In his con‑ demnation of didacticism, however, Mr. Stedman does not include that nobly philosophical strain whose **Beauty is truth,** utterance is often the prophecy of inspira‑ **truth beauty.** tion itself. The didacticism of Pope's "Essay on Man" and of Tennyson's "In Memoriam" are at the extreme poles of the poetic art; the former is a collection of rhymed moral sentiments, resembling poetry only in the outward form, while the latter is the flower of Tennyson's prime, unsurpassed in profound feeling, in chaste beauty, and in imaginative phi‑ losophy. Nor by condemning didacticism does Mr. Stedman exclude from poetry the highest wisdom, that of ethics. He would by no means agree with those who declare that art and morals have nothing in common. Mr. Oscar Wilde has informed the world that a poem is either well-written or ill-written, and that is all there is of it. Be it so, Mr. Stedman might reply; a poem is not well written unless it expresses the highest verities of righteousness. To infuse a "moral" into a work of art is, indeed, to spoil it; but that beauty which is "the unveiled shining counte‑ nance of truth" will always carry a moral, the more effective perhaps in that it is not formally expressed. Baseness in art satiates without satisfying; it does not bear the supreme test of endurance. Indeed, there is no previous writer on the poetic art who grounds it so surely on an ethical, even a religious basis, _{The religious} as Mr. Stedman. In spirit he goes back to ^{basis of poetry.} the time when poetry and the drama were adjuncts of a nation's religion, in that he says: —

" Now the artist not only has a right, but it is his duty, to indulge an anthropomorphism of his own. In his conception the divine power must be the supreme poet, the matchless artist, not only the transcendency, but the immanence of all that is adorable in thought, feeling, and appearance. Grant that the Creator is the founder of rites and institutes and dignities ; yet for the idealist he conceived the sunrise and moonrise, the sounds that ravish, the outlines that enchant and sway. He sets the colors upon the easel, the harp and viol are his invention, he is the model and the clay, his voice is in the story and the song. The love and beauty of women, the comradeship of man, the joy of student-life, the mimic life of the drama as much as the tragedy and comedy of the living world, have their sources in his nature ; nor only gravity and knowledge, but also irony and wit and mirth. Arcady is a garden of his devising. As far as the poet, the artist, is creative, he becomes a sharer of the divine imagination and power, and even of the divine responsibility. "

It is possible that to many this idea may seem daring to the verge of irreverence, but that can be only because it is a thought to which they have _{How reconcil-} not accustomed themselves. No Christian _{able with the-
ology.}

thinker who believes in the immanence of God in his universe, — that in him, according to the apostle, we live and move and have our being, — will discover anything disquieting in this theory of art. Rather will it adjust itself to his theology and to his understanding of the Scriptures with perfect ease, and once comprehended will seem to him the only possible, as well as by far the noblest, conception of the fundamental nature of art.

As to the quality of poetic expression, Mr. Stedman finds nothing to add to Milton's well-known dictum, that it should be simple, sensuous, passionate, — that is to say, impassioned, marked by intensity of emotion. Human passion has always been and probably always will be the theme of poets of the first order. "In truth," says our author, "the potent artist, the great *Poetic expression defined.* poet, is he who makes us realize the emotions of those who experience august extremes of fortune. For what can be of more value than intense and memorable sensations? What else make up that history which alone is worth the name of life?" The most effective expression, however, is not always the fullest expression in words; Browning has shown that the most dramatic effects are produced by the indication of suppressed passion. The poet no more than the actor should "tear a passion to tatters" if he wishes to reach the summit of his art.

The poet, Mr. Stedman holds in conclusion, is not merely a creator, but a prophet. His is a vision not enjoyed by ordinary mortals, and on him is laid the

compulsion to declare it. It is required of him, therefore, that he believe in his prophecy as something
greater than himself. His office is incompatible with
the scepticism that questions whether anything is
certain, whether anything is really worth while.
Neither a cynic nor a pessimist can be a great poet,
for the underlying motive of all strenuous effort and
high achievement is faith. Without such faith, become
vital in action, the highest flight of poetry will not be
essayed, or will be essayed in vain.

To sum up the results of our examination of his
work, we may say that Mr. Stedman seems a clear
case of arrested development, — a man whom hard
fate has bereft of his highest achievement. Poetry is
his native speech. Herein he differs from Mr. Howells,
who, though the writer of very creditable verse, yet
finds in prose his more natural utterance. An artist in
Mr. Stedman hardly ranks among the first verse, not in
prose.
American writers of prose. We are now considering
his style only, — the mere form of his expression, the
dress of his thought. His prose writings are of high
value, but it is a value that does not depend chiefly
on their workmanship. The substance is sterling,
and bears the hall-mark of genuine worth; the form
is conventionally correct, but lacks the unmistakable
stamp of genius. He is, in other words, not the artist
in prose that he is in verse. His style has no serious
faults, but it lacks flavor, sparkle, distinction. His
words do not, " like so many nimble and airy servitors,

trip about him at command." Now almost the contrary, in every particular, may be said of his verse. While he does not rank, by virtue of what he has actually done, with the greatest of our American poets, his verse has a distinct flavor that one would not like to lose. His work, except in that which we may call his juvenile period, could not possibly be mistaken for the work of any other poet. Much of it is not merely free from technical faults, but is imaginative, tender, spirited. It shows genius, and it contains the prophecy of greater things to be áchieved. The unfulfilment of that prophecy will be a serious loss to American letters. Mr. Stedman's place, nevertheless, among American authors can never be anything but a high one. Though his achievement in verse has not yet fulfilled the bright promise of his youth, though His place in his mind is not so opulent or his style so American literature. luxuriant as Lowell's, though he lacks the effervescing wit of Holmes, his actual performance is valuable for its cosmopolitan spirit, its broad culture, its genuine humor, its depth of insight, its conscientious workmanship.

II.

FRANCIS PARKMAN.

AMONG American men of letters, none have a higher rank than the historians. Irving, Prescott, and Motley are names that are not eclipsed by those of Gibbon, Hume, and Macaulay. If Bancroft is not ranked with these, it is not because his labored work is inferior in scholarly research, but because the style, now dry and operose, now turgid and bombastic, puts it distinctly among historical writings of the second class. But there can be no doubt of the right of a fourth American to rank in this company of great historians. By the unanimous suffrages of competent critics, as well as of delighted readers, this honor has been awarded to Francis Parkman.

I.

LIKE Lowell and Holmes, Mr. Parkman belonged to the Brahmin caste of New England. Three generations of ministers were among his ancestors. His father was a pupil of Channing, president of the association of Unitarian ministers, founder of the chair of pulpit eloquence in the theological department of Harvard University, a divine of high repute in his day

for learning, eloquence, and character. It was a
brother of this divine (also a Dr. Parkman,
Of the Brahmin
caste. but Doctor of Medicine, not of Divinity)
who was murdered by his friend, Professor Webster
— one of the most celebrated cases in the history of
American criminal jurisprudence. Francis Parkman
was born in Boston, September 16, 1823, predestined
to the intellectual life. He was graduated at Harvard
in 1844, and for two years thereafter studied law, but
finally abandoned the idea of a professional career.
It does not appear that during his boyhood or his
college days he had shown any strong bent towards
literature. There are singularly few anecdotes or
reminiscences of friends accessible, and the side-lights
that such things often throw on a man's life and work
are quite lacking in his case. One cannot discover
what turned him toward the Great West and decided
his future ; we only know that in 1846 he set out to
explore the Rocky Mountains, and that he lived for
some months among the Dakota Indians and even
wilder tribes, gaining in this way such an intimate
knowledge of aboriginal customs and traditions as few
white men have ever obtained. If it was health that
he sought, this incursion into the wilderness was an
utter failure. The privations that he was compelled
to endure sent him back to civilization with a shattered
frame, and induced an affection of the eyes that would
have ended the literary career of any ordinary man.

The results of this exploration were first given to
the world in a series of articles in " Knickerbocker's

Magazine," and at their conclusion were published in a volume called " Prairie and Rocky Mountain Life " (New York, 1849), which title was afterwards changed into "The California and Oregon Trail," by which name the book has long been known. It is even now delightful reading, and one can faintly imag- The Great ine its fascination for a generation to whom West. the Great West was a region full of mystery and romance. The book was a success in every way, being praised by the critics and proving profitable to the publisher. This decided the author's career, if there was anything left to be decided. It was Mr. Parkman's evident vocation to be a historian, though the state of his health raised a doubt of his ability to follow the call. The field of his labors was also pretty definitely delimited by this first success : it was to be the story of the Indian nations, in their relation to their white conquerors, the English and the French; and this naturally led up to the story of the contest between France and England for the supremacy in North America.

In a steady series the books came from the press, with such breaks only as thorough work required. In 1851 "The Conspiracy of Pontiac" was published, the failure of this conspiracy marking the downfall of the power of the Six Nations. "Pioneers of France in the New World" followed in 1865; His histories. "The Jesuits in North America" in 1867; "La Salle and the Discovery of the Great West" in 1869; "The Old Régime in Canada" in 1874;

"Count Frontenac and New France" in 1877;
"Montcalm and Wolfe" in 1884; and the series was
concluded in 1892 with "A Half Century of Con-
flict." These works fill twelve goodly octavos of some
four hundred pages each, and constitute one of the
notable contributions to historical literature made
during the nineteenth century. The bulk of this
writing proclaims Mr. Parkman to be one of the most
industrious of historians, for it is fully equal to the
great work of Gibbon, and is about twice that of the
histories of Macaulay or Hume. But the mere bulk
of his writing is its least remarkable feature; that
establishes his industry only, and Mr. Parkman was
a man of genius.

II.

By what process of reasoning do we justify the
custom of calling "self-made" him alone who rises
to eminence from poverty? The fact, of course, is
that any man is self-made who is ever made at all.
Wealth and social position may supply the opportunity
of greatness, but they never yet made a man great.
It is a fair matter of debate, indeed, whether wealth
The obstacles   and social distinction are not distinctly un-
of wealth.   favorable to the development of any germ
of greatness with which a man may have the good
fortune to be endowed by nature. There is something
wholesome and bracing in poverty. No great race
has ever been produced in an enervating tropical
climate; the manly virtues flourish in rapidly increas-

ing ratio as we journey away from the equator. The youth who is born with a golden spoon in his mouth and is lapped in luxury from his cradle onward, has not half a chance to make a man of himself. If he turns out a tolerably decent fellow and does a man's work in the world, he has great reason to congratulate himself; while if he proves to be a man of genius and makes all mankind his debtors, something very like a miracle has been wrought. We do well to honor those who have overcome the obstacles of poverty and deficient early training, but let us honor even more those who have conquered the temptations of wealth and the flatteries of society.

Mr. Parkman inherited an ample fortune, and a place in the most cultured and refined circle of Boston was his birthright. He might, without losing the respect of his class, have devoted himself to a life of elegant ease and learned leisure. He might have cultivated any one or all of several gentlemanly and costly tastes. He might have become a bibliomaniac, wise in first editions and fine bindings, or a virtuoso in violins and vases. He might, equally without reproach, have devoted himself to yachting, coaching, or some other of the methods by which the gilded youth of America relieve themselves of their superfluous dollars and kill the time that hangs so heavily on their well-manicured hands. He might His abundant even have become a mere idler, a *bon vivant,* labors. whom everybody calls " a good fellow," — the type of man who is envied by fools and despised by the wise.

Nay, he might have gone to the devil altogether, by the old-fashioned broad road well-travelled of rich young men. He did none of these things. Neither undervaluing nor overvaluing the advantages of wealth and station, he made them the stepping-stones of his career. He labored with a zeal, an industry, an unflagging purpose, not surpassed by men who have to pull hard against wind and tide to get on in life. No mechanic toiling for daily bread has been a harder worker than he. Whether ambition or philanthropy was the spur that urged him on, — and there is no need that we should inquire too curiously, — the spur was at any rate effective.

It is conceded on all hands that Mr Parkman's histories are a contribution of the highest value to our knowledge of early American history. They could not well fail to be this, inasmuch as they traverse a field practically untrodden, and are based on original Originality.   sources. Few readers realize the labor involved in blazing a way through a virgin forest of facts. But Mr. Parkman has done more than blaze a way; he has cleared the forest and brought the land under cultivation. In other words, he has done his work with such thoroughness and minuteness of research, and with such impartiality and accuracy of judgment, that it will not require doing over again for many years to come, if ever. His search has not passed by any material of value known to exist; all the ore in sight has been mined and the veins are exhausted. Until new discoveries are made, little of value remains to be done.

This has involved an immense deal of travel and research at first hand; it has compelled no end of mousing about for hidden and unsuspected sources of knowledge; it prompted numerous visits to France, where the State archives were thrown open to Mr. Parkman's inspection, and their secrets were wrung from them by patient investigation. There was a conscientious thoroughness in this historian's research that would have won men's praise if he had been as robust a man as Macaulay, for example. But this indefatigable worker was not a robust man; His extensive most of his life was passed in a state of researches. health but one degree removed from invalidism. For the greater part of his work he was able to use his own eyes very little; and months at a time he was compelled to spend in a darkened room, in imminent danger of total blindness. Most of his research he was compelled to prosecute by the aid of other eyes than his own, and his books were for the most part composed by dictation. Prescott, it is recorded, in the latter part of his life was afflicted in a similar way, and his brilliant " History of the Conquest of Mexico " was composed in like manner; but Mr. Parkman worked by this method during a period of forty years. Both the extent and the excellence of his work would be remarkable in any case, but are nothing less than astounding in view of these circumstances.

One could hardly mention a parallel case in the whole history of literature. We are accustomed to

think of the composition of " Paradise Lost " and the
other great works that Milton produced in his years
A feat without of blindness, as an unexampled literary
parallel.   feat.   But Milton's task was not to be
named beside Parkman's for difficulty. The composition of an epic, being almost wholly an intellectual process, can be carried on by the help of an
amanuensis with comparative ease.   In historical
writing the mere work of composition is the smallest part of the undertaking. To collect, compare,
and sift the materials is an immense labor, even for
one who has the full use of his eyes, but to depend
on the eyes of others multiplies the difficulty im-
measurably. Take a single instance : one who can
use his own eyes readily acquires the faculty of running his glance rapidly down the page, singling out
the points of interest or value to him and passing by
the rest ; while one who depends on another's eyes
must listen patiently while every word is read to him,
lest he miss something of consequence. In a thousand ways that imagination easily suggests, he is at
a disadvantage, and the demands made on his time
and patience by this method of working are not
easily calculable.

III.

WHOEVER comes after Mr. Parkman can only retell
the same story. It seems unlikely that any discoveries of material remain to be made that will
throw important light on this period of history,

though they may clear up some details and possibly compel modifications of judgment here and there. The substance of the story will remain unchanged. Can any future historian hope to tell it better than Mr. Parkman? Who has ever had the courage to retell Gibbon's story of the decline and fall of the Roman Empire? Much as has been said, and deservedly said, of Mr. Style. Parkman's industry in research, even more may be said, and with no less justice, of his brilliancy of style. Perhaps "brilliant" is not the happiest epithet one could choose, for it may convey to some an implication that the style is unfavorable to strict veracity. Of more than one great historian it has been said, with at least a show of justice, that his style is one in which no man could possibly tell the truth. The historian who affects the grand manner, who makes much use of antithesis and metaphor, who overloads his pages with allusion and quotation, — a historian, in a word, who is chiefly a rhetorician, — is morally certain to be untrustworthy in details. The desire to make an effective sentence will, unconsciously to himself, often prove superior to the desire to tell the truth. Mr. Froude stands a melancholy example for all time of this principle. Mr. Parkman's brilliancy is not rhetorical, in the conventional sense of that term; that is, he does not produce his effects by the free use of the artifices and ornaments of style described and illustrated at length in the standard treatises on rhetoric.

If Mr. Parkman had been a novelist he would be classed as a realist, for he has carried the realistic method into history as no other man of our time has done it. Picturesqueness is a striking feature of his style; his descriptions do not impress one as beautiful, though they are that, but as vivid, and, above all, as truthful. This is precisely what they are. The historian has made his sketch on the spot and from nature, precisely as a painter would do it, and with the same fidelity to detail that a painter would study. A similar method and effect are discernible in all his descriptions of character. Not only Picturesqueness. are the great personages in his pages — Pontiac and La Salle, Montcalm and Wolfe — drawn with wonderful clearness and actually made to live and move before us, but most of the men who receive more than a passing mention are sketched with equal fidelity and effectiveness. As the skilled artist, by a few strokes of the crayon, catches and reproduces the expression of a face with a power that an elaborate oil portrait often fails to equal, so by a phrase or a sentence interjected here and there into his narrative Mr. Parkman has outlined the character of scores of men, and we know them better than through pages of description by most writers.

When the " Saturday Review " praises anything American, we are warranted in concluding that it must be very good indeed. The "Saturday Review" concedes that the writings of Mr. Parkman are certain of a permanent place among the most important historical literature of our age. And it bases its pre-diction, not on the industry and accuracy of the his-torian, but on the excellence of the style. Recognition abroad. It recognizes in him a great artist, as well as a diligent scholar, one who had the instinct of selection, the sense of perspective, the gift of co-ordinating and grouping materials, — in short, the creative power that out of a chaos of facts evolves the cosmos that men call a great historical work. We may pardon the tone of condescension, and even of surprise, in which it is admitted that some good thing does occasionally come out of America, in view of the substantial justice of the verdict. Mr. Parkman's laurels were thus awarded by that con-temporaneous posterity, a foreign nation.

IV.

IT should not be inferred from anything that has been said of Mr. Parkman's methods of work that he was through life a cloistered recluse. On the con-trary, he was a man of the world quite as much as a man of letters. His books alone would warrant the inference that he knew men, that he studied them closely and at first hand, with careful observation of their character and motives. This could never be done by one who shut himself up with books and musty manuscripts. Gibbon has told us, in a some-what celebrated passage, of the help he derived from his service in the militia: " The discipline and evolutions of a modern battalion gave me a clearer notion of the phalanx and the legion; and the captain of the Hampshire grenadiers (the reader may smile) has not been useless to the historian of the Roman Empire." It was no less advantageous to Mr. Parkman to improve his social opportunities. He was always a favorite in Boston society, where his talk was held to be quite as brilliant as his writing. He was also what Dr. Johnson would have termed an eminently " clubbable " man, and for a series of years was president of the far-famed St. Botolph's Club. For many years he was one of the seven corporators of Harvard University, and gave much of his time and thought to the affairs of that institution. By thus keeping in touch with his fellows and his age, he avoided that scholarly aloofness from practical affairs which gives an air of unreality to the work of so many men of letters.

Mr. Parkman was, in fact, one of the few Americans who know how to play as well as how to work. Play — by which one means, of course, any innocent amusement, any exercise of the faculties of body or mind for recreation — has its place in a true philosophy of life, not as a thing permissible merely, but as a duty. It is no more to be disregarded than sleep or the taking of food. It is a thing of which no man need be ashamed, or for which he should apologize. It may be made a vice, just as eating may become gluttony, but play is no

Man of the world.

His play.

more dissipation than rest is laziness. Most adult Americans do not know how to play, and when they take recreation do it in a secret or half shame-faced way. Our men and women are ranging them-selves in two classes, — those who never play and those who never do anything else. It is hard to choose between the incorrigible idler who lives only for pleasure and the incorrigible worker who lives only for his business or profession. It is a wise public sentiment that insists on every man's working, even if he has inherited wealth, but society should add to its law an edict that all men should play also. Those who live long and accomplish much are for the most part men who know how to play. Glad-stone is a famous chopper of trees, and Lord Palmer-ston rode to hounds up to his last years.

It was, perhaps, fortunate for Mr. Parkman that his health compelled him to play, to seek some out-door recreation. He chose horticulture as the secondary business of his life, and as he could do nothing with-out doing it well, he became one of the Horticultural best amateur gardeners of our country, if, pursuits. indeed, he did not rather deserve to be called a pro-fessional. He labored with his own hands at the art, as anybody must who really loves it, no matter how rich he may be, but he also employed his purse liberally in the gratification of what came to be with him a hobby. His residence was surrounded by ample grounds, and in these he had a notable collection of rare and beautiful trees, shrubs, and plants. He was particularly successful in the culture of aquatic plants, and it was largely through his intelligent enthusiasm that amateur gardening has been made a favorite by-pursuit of professional and business men.

It is hardly correct to call Mr. Parkman an amateur gardener, as has already been hinted, though he was never a "professional" in the usual sense of that term, which commonly defines one who is a gardener for revenue only, or mainly. As is almost inevitable in the case of one who handles pen and spade with equal skill, he made literary use of his *His Book of Roses.* horticultural experience, and his "Book of Roses," published in 1866, was highly esteemed among all rosarians, amateur and professional. In 1871 Mr. Parkman was elected professor of horticulture in the agricultural school of Harvard, and filled the chair with eminent ability for two years. Had his health permitted him a longer diversion from the chief work of his life, he would, doubtless, have remained in a position to which his love for the subject would have attracted him so strongly. He was right, however, not to let his play become his work.

At one time it seemed likely that the historian would allow himself another diversion, by making occasional excursions into fiction. In 1856 he published a novel called "Vassall Morton," about which

one can learn little more than the name, the date of
publication, and the fact that the scene of the story
is partly in America and partly in Europe. One
may, perhaps, infer, without more accurate information, that the book was not more than
moderately successful. This was, all things His one novel.
considered, a fortunate circumstance, as a marked
success might have diverted the author's attention
from the work that he has accomplished. Some
fragments of his earlier composition suggest that
Macaulay, had he chosen to devote himself to fiction,
might have made a name as great as that of Scott;
but who would exchange his history for a shelf-full
of romances? And on the other hand, who would
exchange the Waverley novels for a shelf-full of histories? It is well in each case that the shoemaker
stuck to his last, — that the writer faithfully, and even
doggedly, continued to do the kind of work for which,
on the whole, he was best fitted.

Long before his death, we ceased to say of Mr.
Parkman that his best work was probably to come.
On the contrary, the reasonable forecast in his case
seemed to be that his work was substantially done.
The plan of his history was completed, and it was
not likely that he would attempt another enterprise.
We looked upon him as one entitled to spend the
remainder of his days in peace, enjoying the pleasures of society and of nature, honored by all who can
appreciate patient labor, broad scholarship, historic

insight, and a style that illustrates the sparkle, the richness, and the melody of the English tongue. And when he died, though we felt his loss as almost that of a personal friend, we had a serene consciousness that his name is securely enrolled among the immortals.

III.

WILLIAM DEAN HOWELLS.

ONE may easily doubt, though he be never so ardent an advocate of classical study, whether a knowledge of Greek and Latin literature is any essential part of the equipment of a successful man of letters. From the great dramatist who had "small Latin and less Greek" to the latest magazine scribbler, a cloud of witnesses rise up in protest against the idea that college training *The university of authors.* tends to make a man a great writer. Only a graduate of the university of the world has the learning required to become a great poet or a great novelist, and a diploma from any other institution makes no man free of the company of great authors.

> "My only books
> Were woman's looks,
> And folly 's all they 've taught me,"

could be said sincerely only by an incorrigible fool. It is in volumes of this kind — in the keen and constant observation of life, that is to say — that even genius must find its materials, if it is to touch men and move them. Among the most successful of American authors, whether we measure success by immediate popularity, or by substantial achieve-

ment, are striking instances of what, in other callings, we are accustomed to call "self-made men,"
— men who have risen to eminence without that
training in the schools generally-regarded as indispensable. There is probably no more impressive
case of this sort than that of Mr. Howells.

I.

IT is a great thing to be well-born, and an almost
greater thing to be well-bred; happy indeed the
man who is both. The Howells family,
before coming to this country, were
Welsh Quakers, but they show as far back as their
history can be traced an exceptional independence
of sectarian bias. The grandfather of the novelist
was a Methodist, his father was a Swedenborgian,
and Mr. Howells himself would probably be not
unjustly described as a Unitarian. The inheritance of such a tendency to hold lightly denominational bonds, while it would be very unfortunate
for a theologian, might be regarded as a happy
circumstance in the case of one whose calling peculiarly demands the widest and most sympathetic
knowledge of men. There is a place in the world
for ardent sectaries, — nobody who is not a bigot to
liberality will question that; but their place is not
in the ranks of dramatists or novelists.

The father of our novelist was a man of more than
ordinary culture. A printer by trade and an editor

in a small way, he had made quite a large collection of books for his time and for a back-country town. Of the mother we can learn little, but that little indicates a woman of gentle manners and refined tastes. Into such a family a boy was born March 1, 1837, the parents then living at Martin's Ferry, Ohio. Young Howells had the usual education that a boy gets in a country town; beyond the "three R's" it could not reasonably be expected to go. What sort of a boy he was, and what he learned that books could not teach, he A Boy's has himself told us in "A Boy's Town." Town.

This book is the best autobiography of a boy in existence, far less introspective and therefore more truthful than Daudet's "Le Petit Chose," in which the French novelist has told the story of his boyhood pathetically enough, but with too much imagination to make it satisfactory as biography, however one may admire it as literature.

What such a boy would learn at school would necessarily be the least part of his education. He took to reading as naturally as a duck takes to water. His father's library contained a larger proportion of poetry than is common in such collections, and this fact probably had much to do with shaping the first literary ideas of the lad. Like Pope, he "lisped in numbers for the Juvenile numbers came;" or, to state the fact more verse-making. prosaically, while still a small boy he began to make verses, and set them in type himself, in his

father's printing-office. It does not appear whether
the verses found their way into the newspaper then
published by his father, but very likely some of
them did.

The family fortunes were not uniformly good,
country journalism being an even more uncertain
venture then than now. In 1851 there came a
crash. The family took the matter with characteristic philosophy. Mr. Howells says that when
the failure was assured, "we all went down to the
river and went in swimming." Young Howells
then went to work, contributing his earnings — four
dollars a week, as compositor on the Ohio "State
Journal" — to the family purse. Things mended
not long after, and at nineteen he was graduated
from the composing room into journalism. Beginning as an employé of the Cincinnati "Gazette,"
A journalist at   at twenty-two he became news editor of
nineteen.   the Columbus "State Journal," and at
about the same time began his purely literary
career. He did not immediately find his real
vocation, for a time imagining himself called to
be a poet. His first publication was "Poems of
Two Friends" (Columbus, 1860), which he issued
jointly with John J. Piatt, whose acquaintance had
somehow been made during the brief journalistic
experience just described. At about this time the
young poet became a contributor to the "Atlantic
Monthly," then recently founded and on the look-
out for new writers of promise.

In the same year that saw the appearance of this volume of poems Mr. Howells wrote a campaign biography of Abraham Lincoln that did admirable service. Except in the West, The biographer of Lincoln. Lincoln was, at the time of his nomination, comparatively unknown to his own party; and when the news was flashed along the wires the general exclamation was, "Who is Abe Lincoln?" This book did much to make the candidate known, and it furnished newspaper editors and campaign orators plenty of material for the answering of all questions regarding the party's candidate. For this service the biographer received one hundred and sixty dollars, and later on, in accordance with time-honored custom, there was added an appointment from President Lincoln as consul at Venice.

The use made of both rewards was characteristic. The money was expended upon a trip to Boston *via* Montreal, — a route which Mr. Howells turned to excellent account afterwards in "Their Wedding Journey." This was a red-letter date in the budding author's history, for on this visit he made the personal acquaintance of Lowell, Holmes, and others whom he had previously known only by reputation or through correspondence. One will not go far astray in regarding this visit as having determined the course of his life thereafter. The consulship at Venice was likewise made Consul at Venice. to contribute to the broadening of knowledge and sympathies, — every forward step that the young author gained becoming the vantage-ground for a still further advance. If the spoils system in our diplomatic service produced more frequently such results as these, one could look upon it with a greater degree of toleration. But the pocket boroughs were not saved in England by the fact that Macaulay and Burke owed to them their first seats in Parliament; and the appointment of Hawthorne and Howells to discharge political debts cannot save the spoils system.

The years from 1861 to 1865 were spent in acquiring the Italian language, in study of the national literature, and in travel. No complaint was ever made that the consul failed to perform his duty in Venice satisfactorily, but he certainly found time to extend his education vastly in these

Venetian Life and Italian Journeys. four years. His "Venetian Life" (London and New York, 1866) and "Italian Journeys" (Boston, 1867) were the first-fruits of this residence abroad. Two more delightful and instructive books about Italy have never been published, and they still deservedly find a host of appreciative readers. We may not improbably ascribe to this foreign residence and· travel a certain cosmopolitan spirit, a breadth of "atmosphere," as painters say, that is characteristic of the work of later years.

On returning to this country in 1866, Mr. Howells was for a time a writer for the "New York Tribune" and the "Nation," but was soon offered the post of assistant editor of the "Atlantic Monthly" by James T. Fields, and in 1872 became editor of that magazine. In this position he served with complete acceptance and success, until his resignation in 1881 in order to devote himself more completely to original literary work. In many respects he made a model magazine editor. He was painstaking, enterprising, courteous, and firm.

Editor of the Atlantic.

He did not forget, in his sympathy with the writer struggling for a hearing, that the patrons of the magazine had a prior right to the best literature to be got, whether in prose or verse. Without breaking with past tradition, he introduced fresh features and infused new life and spirit into every department of the magazine. In spite of the contempt he may even then have felt and has since expressed for critics and criticism, he made the critical work of "The Atlantic" a force in current literature. He established the "Contributors' Club," — a sort of free parliament for the expression of opinion on a wide range of topics by some of the cleverest of American writers. In a word, if he had not preferred to be the representative American novelist of his day, he might have become its representative editor. He has all the gifts of a great journalist, except, perhaps, lack of conscientious scruple. With long and patient effort — who knows? — he might have acquired even that.

II.

WITH the publication of "Their Wedding Journey" in 1871, Mr. Howells entered on his real
Their Wed-   career.   Hitherto he had been experi-
ding Journey. menting, now he had found his vocation.
One cannot treat his poems as anything better
than the exercises of a clever lad, or the amuse-
ments of a versatile man of letters.   His critical
work is a by-product, a collection of chips from
the workshop of a busy writer.   From this time
on we have to do with a man who is first of all and
last of all a novelist.   Novel after novel has made
its appearance, with the unfailing regularity of the
seasons.   Yet this fecundity has not been reached
at the expense of quality.   None of his books bears
marks of undue haste, of careless workmanship, of
failing powers.   On the contrary, if each book
published has not surpassed all its predecessors,
we can trace in the author from year to year an
increase of power, a completer mastery of the resources of his art, a larger view, an ampler spirit.
One has heard and read that of late years a change
has come over Mr. Howells, — that the romance of
his earlier books has faded away into a hard, dry,
His alleged later realism, that he has lost the joyousness
pessimism.   of youth and has become pessimistic, not
to say cynical.   This seems an opinion founded on a
partial and superficial knowledge of Mr. Howells's

writings. There is nothing more romantic or idyllic in the Marches when we first meet them on "Their Wedding Journey" than when after a score of years we renew their acquaintance in "A Hazard of New Fortunes." Such change as is to be noted in his later books is due rather to the influence of the much-admired Tolstoï than to any other cause. "The World of Chance" is quite strongly tinged with the Russian novelist's views of society and religion. It cannot be said, however, that much of the light of hope is thrown on the regeneration of society by a book in which one would-be regenerator becomes a maniac, and commits suicide after unsuccessfully attempting murder, while another dies without having accomplished the great purpose of his life, the publication of a book that was to be the gospel of a new era.

III.

EVEN a casual reader of these books is soon aware that their author is no mere story-teller, content just to amuse the public, regarding their smiling approval as the be-all and end-all of his obligation. He is a thoroughly instructed artist, who works not at haphazard, who succeeds not by lucky strokes of genius, but proceeds according to a well-defined theory of his art, — a theory that we must take pains to understand if we would judge him fairly and sympathetically. We may dissent from the theory, we may find the practice faulty; what we may not do is to judge him in the empirical and *a priori* fashion so common in current criticism.

Both in theory and in practice, Mr. Howells is a realist. He believes, that is to say, that the chief end of the novel is not to tell a story, but to represent life. A story there must be, of course, but not necessarily a plot; the history of the spiritual development of a single personage, for example, is a "story." The novel must tell a story in the sense that a picture tells a story, and in no other sense; in other words, whatever represents a bit of life necessarily tells a story. This fundamental canon requires no debate, for it is not merely truth but truism, or nearly so. Like Captain Cuttle's observation, the bearings of it lie in its application, and it is when Mr. Howells begins to apply his canon, whether in his own practice or in criticism of others, that doubts begin to suggest themselves.

Howells a realist.

Art is necessarily selective, for the sufficient reason that no man can represent the whole of life. It is only a scrap of landscape that the painter can put on his largest canvas, and only a glimpse of some tiny segment of the social cosmos (or shall we say chaos?) can be afforded the readers of a three-volume novel. This being the case, the question immediately arises whether some principle or principles should not govern the selection of what is to be represented. There are professors of realism in fiction who teach that all possible objects are equally worthy of representation. They do not really believe this, because even they practise selection, and therefore, of course, rejection; but, as children say, they "make believe" believe it when they are challenged. Nay, they virtually affirm that the more worthless and commonplace, the more hideous and repulsive and vile an object is, the more worthy it is of representation.

True realism and false.

Now this application of the canon of realism one is certainly entitled to dispute without thereby incurring suspicion of questioning the canon itself. All art has taken it for granted, from its rudest beginnings until now, that some objects in nature, some experiences in life, are better adapted for representation than others. The choice of object has been dictated, in the main, by its capacity to please. Without disputing the fact that there is a place in art for the grotesque, for the painful, even, its chief function is to please and ennoble. The great artists have always appealed to the moral as well as to the æsthetic faculties. One is not convinced, therefore, by any assertions or examples of realists in fiction, that the trivial and the vile furnish proper subjects for the artist. To the healthy mind they give no pleasure; they inspire only *ennui* or disgust.

Mr. Howells cannot be too promptly acquitted of any suspicion of choosing the vile as subject of his

art. His one villain, Bradley Hubbard, is so ill
done, in comparison with his other work, as to
suggest lack of knowledge of this type. The bad
woman he has never attempted to draw, though
American society is not quite guiltless of Becky
Sharps. But the trivial, the commonplace, he has
exhibited in season and out, especially in his repre-
The gospel of sentations of American women. That,
trivial common-
place. however, introduces a subject so large as
to demand discussion by itself. Passing it by for
the present, it is pertinent to inquire, Can it be
that Mr. Howells gives us in his books a fair
representation of life as he has known it? Has
his whole experience been of this stale, flat, unprofitable sort? Has he never known anybody who
had a soul above buttons? The thing seems difficult to believe. It may be that the people we meet
in his novels are those with whom he is most
familiar, those that he feels himself most competent to depict, but that they exhaust his experience of life and his knowledge of the world one
cannot so easily accept.

Let us be just, however. To Mr. Howells we
must award the praise of having done well what he
set out to do. Given the propriety of the choice, we
must grant that he has made a faithful and lifelike
picture of the thing chosen. It is with the choice
itself that many of his readers quarrel; or, perhaps
one should say, they quarrel with his persistent
and exclusive choice of one type of character and

one sort of experience for representation in his fiction. Whether he has not known higher types of character among us, or has lacked courage to attempt their portraiture — in either case he has chosen badly for his readers, though possibly prudently for himself.

IV.

No examination of the works of Mr. Howells would have any claim to comprehensiveness that failed to take account of his farce-comedies. There is quite a series of these, beginning with "The Sleeping-Car" and ending with the "Unexpected Guests." No American author has given us more admirable fooling than this, at once clever and refined. The humor is free from that element of exaggeration supposed to be peculiarly characteristic of American humor. The humor of Mr. Howells is as well-bred and studiously proper as the elegant Bostonians who are his *dramatis personæ;* it is humor in a swallow-tail coat and white-lawn tie, so to say. Those *dramatis personæ* deserve a separate word: they are but four, — the real characters, that is to say, though make-weights may occasionally be introduced, — but they have been ingeniously utilized, year after year, in new situations, until they seem to us people whom we have known all our lives. The same idea has been almost simultaneously worked out by several clever writers of short stories;[1] but none of his rivals has succeeded like Mr. Howells in making his people real flesh-and-blood persons.

These comedies bring us again face to face with the chief grievance one has against Mr. Howells, and it is time to have it fairly out with him, — that The caricature is, his curiously and indeed exasperat- of American womanhood. ingly inadequate portraiture of American womanhood.　This is more or less a fault of all his writing, but it becomes most conspicuous in these farces.　Are Mrs. Roberts and Mrs. Campbell fair types of American womanhood?　Is the American woman who is both well-bred and well-read usually only one remove from idiocy?　Is she habitually so silly and flighty as to suggest that her proper place is in some institution for the feeble-minded?　One does not dispute that the originals of Mesdames Roberts and Campbell exist — unfortunately, one has met them; one only pities the man who has been so unspeakably unfortunate as to meet nobody else.　The plea that they exist is not a valid defence to our accusation, — Nana and Madame Bovary and Sappho exist also, without doubt; the charge being that there has been a failure in literary perspective, an artistic blunder of which even a demonstration of realistic

[1] Notably by Mr. Thomas A. Janvier in his " Color Studies " of artist life in New York, and by Mr. Richard Harding Davis in his portraiture of Van Bibber, the New York young man about town.

truth furnishes no justification. Art is something different from and higher than photography.

Mr. Howells is inclined to wave aside such criticism with a rather jaunty air, pronouncing it "extremely comical" as he does so. "I once said," so he is reported as remark- *The author "confesses and avoids."* ing, "to a lady who asked me, 'Why don't you give us a grand, noble, perfect woman?' that I was waiting for the Almighty to begin. I think that women, as a rule, are better and nobler than men, but they are not perfect. I am extremely opposed to what are called ideal characters. I think their portrayal is mischievous; it is altogether offensive to me as an artist, and, as far as the morality goes I believe that when an artist tries to create an ideal he mixes some truth up with a vast deal of sentimentality, and produces something that is extremely noxious as well as nauseous. I think that no man can consistently portray a probable type of human character without being useful to his readers. When he endeavors to create something higher than that, he plays the fool himself and tempts his readers to folly. He tempts young men and women to try to form themselves upon models that would be detestable in life, if they were ever found there."

Mr. Howells makes the form of plea known to lawyers as "confession and avoidance." He admits that the women of his fictions are imperfect, but throws the responsibility on the Almighty, — he

has given us faithful portraits of the kind of women
he has found in the world.   The validity of this defence can be admitted only by those who find it cred-

The plea not   ible.   His women, taken as a class, com-
valid.   prise more varieties of the species fool
than most of us have known by actual experience;
but that he has never in his life, as son, husband,
father, friend, come in contact with any other sort
of woman than this mixture of superficial accomplishments and frivolous mind, — this, as A. Ward
feelingly remarked, is "2 mutch."   The ideal
heroine of fiction is not a creature as

> "beautiful as sweet,
> And young as beautiful, and soft as young,
> And gay as soft, and innocent as gay,"

and silly as all the rest put together, because this
is not the best type of woman in real life.

The plea of Mr. Howells must, therefore, be
overruled; he cannot be absolved from the guilt of
defective art by the plea that the art is perfect, and
that the defect is in womankind.   The plea contains
as little of truth as of gallantry.   And by saying
this, one intends no impeachment of the novelist's
sincerity.   Mr. Howells takes himself and his art
with great seriousness, and honestly believes in
both with all his might.   He is merely the victim
of misplaced confidence in this instance.   It were
treason to American women to accept his lame
and impotent conclusion that they are fit only to

chronicle small beer. It were to believe the future of our country hopeless.

> "For she that out of Lethe scales with man
> The shining steps of Nature, shares with man
> His nights, his days, moves with him to one goal,
> Stays all the fair young planet in her hands, —
> If she be small, slight-natured, miserable,
> How shall men grow?"

Justice requires the admission that Mr. Howells has shown signs of late of strengthening this weak place in his stories. It is always the unexpected that happens, and in his "World of Chance" he has at last given us a *The World of Chance.* heroine who is neither idiotic nor feeble-minded. One says "heroine," since that is the conventional term for the chief female character of a novel. In the strictest sense of the word, Peace Hughes is not a heroine at all; she is something far better than that, a genuine woman. Her station is not exalted, her like may be found by anybody who takes a walk on Broadway, — her like in all outward characteristics, one means. Her father is a socialistic "crank," and she is a stenographer and typewriter in a publishers' office. Mr. Howells does not represent her as saying or doing a single heroic thing, — anything that surpasses the experience of a thousand young women in New York; yet he has drawn her with so much sympathy, so much fidelity, as to make her the strongest and best woman in all his fictions.

Mr. Howells deserves congratulations on his discovery of this type of woman.   If he will continue
to live in New York and to use his eyes he will
discover other types not less womanly.
A woman at last.   One does not demand impossibilities of
him in protesting against the inanities of his previous books.   Latter-day readers have no great
liking for the angelic or the heroic type of woman
that novelists used to give us.   It is doubtless our
misfortune, but most of us never yet have happened
to meet either of those types.   The women we have
known were neither angels nor heroines, but just
women.   The greater part of them have not been
fools.   The realistic method of Mr. Howells shows
to best advantage when, as in this book, he applies
it to the delineation of a real woman, in no way
exceptional, unless it be in a certain delicacy and
nobleness of nature.   For one cannot think so well
of the world as to believe that women like Peace
Hughes âre common.

V.

IF that country is most fortunate that has no
annals, may we not count happiest that author of
whose life there is little to record save the titles of
his books?   This is practically the case with Mr.
Howells since 1881; but of these records there
is a long series.   No author has afforded us an
example of systematic and industrious labor at his
art more highly to be commended.   It is something

to have set before our young people who cherish
literary aspirations, as on the whole the most prosperous of American writers, a man who claims no
peculiar exemptions from moral obligation on the
score of genius, who is as regular at his desk as
any blacksmith at his anvil, who is blameless in
every private and public relation. Mr. Howells has
found time, by virtue of this system and diligence,
not only to produce a novel every year, but to do
a considerable quantity of other literary Howells's by-
work. Among these by-products, as they products.
have already been called, may be specified the editing, with critical introductions, of a series of volumes called "Choice Biographies" (8 vols. Boston,
1877-8); the volume of critical essays on "Modern
Italian Poets" (1887); and his papers contributed
to the Editor's Study of "Harper's Magazine,"
the best of which have been collected in "Criticism
and Fiction" (New York, 1891).

It is not a little funny to read in these criticisms
denunciations of critics, so fierce in matter, in
phrases so urbane. One suspects that His quarrel
Mr. Howells would like to be rude to the with the critics.
critics if he only knew how, he labors so hard to
say something cutting, something that will pierce
the notoriously thick hide of this terrible wild
beast. For your critic is essentially a devourer of
authors, and can no more be credited with good intentions than a tiger. It is doing the critic undeserved honor, this comparing him to a tiger, for Mr.

Howells will allow him to be nothing higher in the scale of being than a parasite. "The critic exists," he tells us, "because the author first existed. If books failed to appear, the critic must disappear like the poor aphis or the lowly caterpillar in the absence of vegetation." This sort of thing, diluted through many pages, does less to convince the public than to convict the writer. Is it the galled jade that winces? Has the critic's lash been so vigorously wielded as to cause Mr. Howells pain commensurate with this retaliation? Be this as it may, he must be held to have a very defective conception of the critic's function. One is astonished, if he rate this function so low, that he is willing to enact the parasite himself. Shall one who proclaims from the housetops that the clown's part is unworthy of a man, presently don the motley and himself play the fool?

The critic, rightly considered, is not a parasite but a middleman. His function in literature is as
The critic's function legitimate.   valid and as useful as the merchant's in commerce. Short-sighted men have denounced the merchant as a parasite on the body politic, their ground being that he is not a producer and gains his living at the expense of those who add to the world's wealth; his suppression has therefore been demanded as an act of justice to the world's real workers. But the more philosophical economist has shown that the merchant does produce value, by taking goods from the place where

they are not wanted to the place where consumers demand them. The critic who understands his business and pursues it honestly is a literary producer, no less than the author; he finds a market, that is, appreciative readers, for works that otherwise might never be heard of, and thus adds something of substantial value to literature. One need not maintain that the critic's function is coördinate with that of the author, that the critic produces what is as valuable as the masterpiece of poet or philosopher, to make good his right of existence. Who shall say that Addison, in his series of papers on Milton, did not produce something of real, yes, of high value to letters? If it were not for the makers of paper and ink the author himself would soon vanish, "like the poor aphis or the lowly caterpillar;" but shall the worthy mechanics and tradesmen who supply these materials of the scribbling art be privileged to insinuate that authors are no better than parasites? Go to, they shall be roundly rebuked if they are guilty of such presumption, and that by Mr. Howells himself.

It is a vain fight on which Mr. Howells has entered, even were he thrice-armed by having his quarrel strictly just. The sons of Zeruiah A contest vain be too hard for him. The critics grow at best. apace. Their name is legion, their spirit Ishmaelitish, their activity incessant, their prolificacy portentous. It is easy to flout them, as Mr. Howells has done, — as Disraeli did when, with mordant sarcasm, he defined a critic as an author who has failed; or as Byron, when, smarting under the lash of Jeffrey he wrote, with wit vitriolic:—

> " A man must serve his time to every trade
> Save censure — critics all are ready made.
> Take hackney'd jokes from Miller, got by rote,
> With just enough of learning to misquote;
> A mind well skill'd to find or forge a fault,
> A turn for punning, call it attic salt; . . .
> Fear not to lie, 't will seem a lucky hit;
> Shrink not from blasphemy, 't will pass for wit;
> Care not for feeling — pass your proper jest,
> And stand a critic, hated yet caressed."

Obviously Jeffrey might have retorted that Byron showed his own confidence in the recipe by following it exactly, but the critic is notoriously easy to be cowed into meekness when the baited author turns upon him, and so Jeffrey missed this chance. On the whole, have not the flock of harried authors had their fair revenge on the critics? Most of the latter would never have been known to posterity had they not been "damned to everlasting fame" in some immortal work, as the fly is sometimes preserved in the precious drop of amber.

Still let us maintain that the critic is a harmless, and even a useful, animal. Like a certain
Not so black other great personage he is not so black
as painted. as he is generally painted. The author is often unjust to him, and sometimes — let us be honest now — he is even more unjust to himself. Criticism is not the last refuge of incompetence.

It is not fault-finding, though both critic and author are but too prone to forget this essential truth. A critic, as the etymology of the word implies, is a judge, — one who weighs evidence, who impartially examines, discerns, separates, distinguishes. It is no less the office of the judge to acquit the innocent than to convict the guilty. It is a small part, and the most disagreeable part, of criticism to point out defects; the more agreeable as well as the more important work is to recognize beauties and to help others see them. The critic has already been compared to the merchant, but an apter analogy is perhaps suggested by the *cicerone.* It is his business to point out to others the places of interest, the strokes of genius, the felicitous achievements in literary art, in the work under review, and thus assist others to form a just and intelligent judgment as to its total merits. Nor does it avail for the author sneeringly to challenge the critic to prove his competence by producing superior work. The critic may reply, in the saying of Didacus Stella, that a dwarf standing on the shoulders of a giant may see farther than the giant himself.

Anybody can find fault, — anybody, at least, who has a small soul, a feeble wit, and a bitter tongue. To criticise, in the true sense, is not within the powers of everybody. It demands a large soul, a trained mind, a catholic taste, a teachable disposition, — a sweet reasonableness,

Criticism not fault-finding.

5

to use the phrase of Matthew Arnold. The just judge must sometimes pronounce sentence against an offender; even Mr. Howells has shown us that, when he condemns so gently the rabid critic. Bad work must be pronounced what it is, for the critic, like every other honest man, must strive to keep "alight that little spark of celestial fire — conscience." But the critic who recognizes the true dignity and responsibility of his office will be at least as hearty in recognition of good work as in condemnation of bad; his praises will be bestowed quite as freely as his blame, and with greater evident pleasure, for he will always rejoice when his conscience absolves him from the duty of censure, and warrants him in inviting a warm but discriminating admiration for the work under review. He will, however, shun, as he would shun the plague, indiscriminate praise or blame. He will regard gush as only one degree less culpable than slander; for to bear false witness in favor of one's neighbor is only one step above bearing false witness against him. In short, he will try to speak the truth, as any honest man should, neither less nor more. It will, of course, be the truth as he sees it that he will speak, colored more or less, unavoidably, by his peculiar training, prepossessions, and acquired beliefs; and

"A fool must now and then be right by chance."

But better than speak the truth as he sees it, can no man do — except recognize the limits of his intelligence, the fallibility of his judgments and the equal presumptive honesty of those who differ from him. It is in this last particular that many critics, otherwise well equipped, grievously fail.

Enough, with over-measure, of this. Let Mr. Howells, if he will, renounce the critic and all his works, and in the next breath do the same works and greater things also. We do not demand of him that consistency which is the virtue of feeble minds, but are rather grateful to find in him a single redeeming vice. Even though he occasionally aggravate us by his wrong-headedness, as some of us must consider it, Mr. Howells is easily the first living American novelist. We cannot deny him the praise of being faithful to his own ideal, of practising diligently his own canons of art. He himself tells us, with great earnestness and frequent iteration, that he utterly contemns and rejects the notion that the novel should aim merely to entertain. What we must say to any serious fiction is this, "Is it true? true to the motives, the impulses, the principles that shape the life of actual men and women?" If the answer be in the affirmative, such a work cannot be bad, for this truth "necessarily includes the highest morality and the highest artistry." To realize this ideal, Mr. Howells has earnestly striven. If he has failed in some instances to reach it, his failure is not due to lack of conscientious industry and high resolve. And certainly, within his limitations, of all our American writers none has come nearer to doing in fiction what the greatest master of the drama has declared to be the purpose of the stage, "to hold as 't were the mirror up to nature; to show virtue her own feature, scorn her own image, and the very age and body of the time his form and pressure."

IV.

HENRY JAMES.

"ISOCRATES adviseth Demonicus," says quaint old Burton, "when he came to a strange city, to worship by all means the gods of the place." If you go to Boston, you must be prepared to do homage to Henry James. One who is not ready to make this author his idol may yet freely admit that he is not *une quantité négligeable.* We may love him, or we may detest him; ignore him, we cannot.

I.

ALMOST two decades ago Bayard Taylor wrote, apropos of some of Mr. James's earlier work: "Few men have been so brilliantly equipped for literary performance. Carefully trained taste, large acquirements of knowledge, experience of lands and races, and association with the best minds, have combined to supply him with all the purely intellectual requisites which an author could desire." This is Brilliantly praise that is no more than scrupulously equipped. just to one who was born, if ever an American novelist was, under a lucky star. His father, distinguished during his lifetime as Henry James, senior, was a philosopher and theological writer of considerable note, — the inheritor of an ample fortune from his father, a merchant of Albany, N. Y.; a graduate of Union College in 1840, and afterward a student at Princeton; by turns orthodox Presbyterian, Sandemanian, Swedenborgian, Spiritualist; a man who boxed the compass of theological belief retaining still the personal regard of all who knew him. Henry James, junior, was born in New York City, in 1843. His education was altogether out of the common; little of it was according to ordinary methods, and all was conducted under his father's personal supervision; begun in America, after 1855 it was carried on and completed abroad, at Geneva, Paris, Boulogne-sur-Mer, and Bonn. What little he learned in the Harvard Law School, which he entered in 1862, does not require this statement to be modified, one supposes, for the law was with him never a serious purpose.

Into the nature of this education there is no need to inquire, since its fruits are so evident in Mr. James's writings. It may have been less or more than an equivalent of the scholastic lore of an ordinary university course; it certainly included an intimate Knowledge of acquaintance with several modern languages and a comprehensive knowledge of their literatures. It also comprised such a minute familiarity with foreign society, with European customs and ways of thinking, as probably no other American novelist has had. Mr. Howells has certainly made good use of his opportunities abroad, but he has not that minute knowledge of foreigners that is

shown by the author of " The American." Mr. Crawford may know Italy better than Mr. James, but he
does not know France with anything like the latter's
thoroughness, nor England either, for the matter of
that. Indeed, it is not saying too much to assert that
long residence abroad has made Mr. James more
European than American. Since 1869 he has spent
most of his time between England and France. This
has given him peculiar qualifications for originating a
new type of fiction. Fortunately for his fame, he has
not attempted to represent a society of which he knows
comparatively little. In the few cases in which he has
chosen an American scene for his story he has selected
his locality with discretion, and has relied _{Lack of famil-}
for his chief characters on foreigners and _{America.}
travelled Americans. The American abroad he has
studied with great care and attention to detail; the
American at home he may almost be said not to know.
Whether one likes the flavor of his books or not, one
cannot fail to distinguish it from that of any other
American novelist.

II.

THE new species of fiction originated by Mr. James
has been named the International Novel. We may
take " The American" (Boston, 1877), _{The Interna}
" Daisy Miller" (New York, 1878), " The _{tional Novel.}
Portrait of a Lady" (Boston, 1881), and " The Princess
Casamassima" (London and New York, 1886), as the
best examples of his work in its various periods. In his

earlier books he was a preacher of social righteousness. His theme was the contrast between American and European life and manners, greatly to the disadvantage of American manners and ideals, in many cases. The American, in the book of that title, is a man in middle life who has "made his everlasting fortune," and has gone to Europe to enjoy it, with some vague idea of marriage as a part of the enjoyment. He is a very good specimen of the "self-made" American, not too much inclined to worship his maker, by no means vulgar in his tastes, rather intellectual and artistic in a crude, untaught way, not loud or aggressive in manner, appreciating himself at his full value, yet modest withal, clean in morals, and unsophisticated in

The American. Parisian viciousness, — in short, a gentleman at the core, though lacking some of the graces and polish demanded by "society." This Mr. Newman, while he does not quite believe money to be omnipotent, firmly believes that it will accomplish most things, and has no doubt that it will buy his way into the good graces of any foreigner. He falls in love with a young French widow, of noble family, — a family anxious for reasons of their own that she shall marry a second time, and marry a rich man. He becomes engaged to her, with her family's consent, but the noble marquis and his mother (who rule the family) are so overwhelmed with chagrin when they fully realize what a social gulf separates the American from them that they break off the match. The widow obeys her mother, though heart-broken, and retires to a convent.

Newman obtains proofs that the marquis and his mother are base and even criminal, threatens to expose them, but finally relents and burns the documents; and in this tangled state of things the story reaches its conclusion with nothing concluded. In Daisy Miller we have the female counterpart of Newman, — the young woman who is as good as gold, so sure of herself that she never once dreams anybody can doubt her; who, nevertheless, does all Daisy Miller. manner of risky things, that in any girl of European training and traditions would indicate total depravity, but are in her only a combination of ignorance and wilfulness.

One cannot deny that these two books are realistic in every detail. There are Newmans and Daisy Millers in Europe, — the type was more common, perhaps, a decade ago than now, — there are Americans more vulgar still, who do not stop with innocently doing compromising and *outré* things, but are shamelessly vicious. No doubt the American girl abroad deserved the sharp rebuke conveyed in "Daisy Miller;" her male counterpart was let off very easily, on the whole, in " The American." If one quarrels with Mr. James it must be on the ground of what he has not said, rather than of what he has said. His half-truths. He has told the truth, — that is to say, he has told a part of the truth. This is at once his justification and the chief ground of complaint against him; for in fiction, as everywhere else, one feels —

" That a lie hich is half a truth is ever the blackest of lies."

Why, one asks again and again, has not Mr. James told the other half of the truth? Why has he never depicted the American gentlewoman and gentleman abroad, cultivated, polished, courteous, refined? That is a type which exists as truly as the other, and is quite as worthy of representation; nor is it beyond the powers of Mr. James to represent it adequately. He knows and doubtless appreciates the American cosmopolite, of both sexes, and his art would be truer if it had been more comprehensive. The angry criticism roused by "Daisy Miller" was not, therefore, wholly that are whole unjust, but it was right rather as the exlies. pression of healthy instincts than as a result of intelligent comprehension. People vaguely felt that the book was unjust to America, and that the author was unpatriotic. In this they were wrong; but complaint may be made with at least a show of justice against Mr. James for letting the book stand all these years without supplement.

In some of his books, it might be replied in behalf of Mr. James, he has represented the polished American. But this is only partly true; he has, indeed, given us admirable portraits of the Europeanized American, notably in "The Europeans" and "The Portrait of a Lady," but hardly of the genuine American. We certainly have among us men and women who, without having lost the racy quality of Western character, have acquired the culture and manner that mark well-bred people the world over. An English gentleman, a French gentleman, has a distinct flavor of his own, and is in many ways a more interesting personage than a cosmopolite whose nationality cannot be inferred from his speech or notions. An American gentleman should have the same attractiveness for the observer, and should furnish equally good material for the novelist's art. This is a type, however, for which one will search in vain through the novels of Mr. James. One finds it difficult to understand why it should have been so persistently avoided by a writer so well fitted to depict it. Mr. James's art has suffered by his persistent preaching of the gospel according to Europe. One is willing to make the acquaintance of any number of Europeans, and even of Europeanized Americans, — in novels, — provided there is not constantly obtruded upon him the moral : " You are in all things less than the least of these, — except, perhaps, in native goodness, which does n't count."

A missing type.

Possibly Mr. James has himself concluded that he has said quite enough on this subject, for in some of his more recent books, notably in " The Princess Casamassima," he has ignored his countrymen altogether. The result is that, having no lesson to inculcate, no warning to deliver, his story becomes charming. Mr. James in general scouts the idea that a story need have a plot. There is, he would say, no orderly and logical sequence of events in every-day life, and why should there be such sequence in fiction? He is equally contemptuous, in a general way, of that sentiment which demands of

Signs of improvement.

a novelist heroic actions on the part of his characters. He has in effect, if not in set terms, declared it to be imperfect art when an author is forced to disentangle the thread of his tale by recourse to murder or suicide or any other catastrophe. But not even Mr. James can practise this theory of the novelist's art with entire consistency. In the book last mentioned he panders to the unlawful desires of the ordinary novel-reader by providing something that may almost be called a plot; he introduces incidents that in any other writer we should unhesitatingly call romantic; and he concludes his tale with a suicide and the most approved blood-curdling concomitants. Surely there is reason to hope that in the course of a few more years he may in practice, if not in word, subscribe to Mr. Crawford's declaration of faith, and refuse to be called either realist or romancer.

III.

THE art of fiction is not confined to the writing of novels; it includes also the Short Story. This is

The Short Story.

a comparatively new species of literature, by no means to be confounded with the Tale, of which so excellent specimens may be found in the "Decameron" and "Heptameron" by those who can stomach those books. There were heroes before Agamemnon, and there have been spinners of yarns before those of the present day. But the

short story of the period is not a mere tale, beginning nowhere in particular, and going on until the
narrator's breath or the hearer's patience fail; it
has as definite rules of composition as a novel or an
epic. It has a distinct purpose, and that purpose
is accomplished by a well-regulated advance, every
step of which is calculated with the nicest art.
There is no master of this species of composition, on the whole, comparable to Mr. James, at
least among American writers; and in this branch
of the art of fiction American writers surpass all
others save only the French. The short story
has always been a striking feature of our literature. Nothing better in this kind of writing has
been produced than Irving's "Legend _{Americans mas-}
of Sleepy Hollow," Poe's "Gold Bug," _{ters of this art.}
and the "Twice Told Tales" of Hawthorne. In
England the short story has languished. The
"Christmas Stories" of Dickens are perhaps the
best specimens that "the tight little isle" can
boast, though some of the work of Charles Reade
and Wilkie Collins is not far inferior. But the
best of these stories lack the artistic perfection our
American writers have achieved. The great English
novelists either wrote short stories but seldom, like
Thackeray, or not at all, like Scott. The British
intellect seems to find difficulty in turning itself
around in less than the orthodox three-volume
space.

It was the good fortune of Mr. James to begin

his career at the very time when American periodi-
Authors must live. cal literature was entering on its most
rapid stage of development.   A market
was thus provided for short stories such as had
never been known before.   Now, authors no more
than other producers will keep on making unsalable
goods, and the periodical press is a necessary condition of prolific production of short stories, because
it affords a market for them on a large scale, — a
scale hitherto unexampled in the history of literature.   Even an author must live.   Or, if the stern
critic reply, *à la* Talleyrand, "Pardon me, I do not
see the necessity," he will at least accept the statement with this amendment, — an author must live if
he is to go on producing.   And even if he is otherwise provided with the means of living than by
payment for his writing, — as one conjectures may
have been the case with Mr. James, — still, he will
not, unless he is one of a thousand, go on writing
unless he has some encouragement from the public
to do so.   He is doubly fortunate if he receives
sufficient recognition to encourage him to proceed,
yet is freed from the temptation to do hasty work
for the sake of turning out "pot-boilers."

Mr. James appears to have been thus independent
of the pecuniary rewards of his pen at the outset of
Requirements of the Short Story. his career.   He did not need to make of
his stories mere "pot-boilers."   He early
discovered that this species of writing demands
capacity and training of a peculiar order, as any one

else is likely to discover who sits down and tries to write a story by the light of nature. Power of invention, fertility of imagination, and facility of style are indispensables, but the first requisites are sense of proportion, and lucidity of vision. In the short story there must be no fumbling with a purpose, no hazy observation, no indecisive movement; all must be sure, well-devised, clean-cut.

There are no stories of this sort more workmanlike than those of Mr. James; witness the volume entitled "A Passionate Pilgrim," composed wholly of these tales. Witness other volumes of the same character, and numerous stories in the magazines not gathered into volumes. "Workmanlike" one calls these stories; a little too workmanlike, perhaps, they are at times. The author is so delighted with the perfection of skill he has attained that he now and then invites us, as it were, to Too clever by half. admire his cleverness. His air seems to say, "See how thoroughly I understand my trade, and how neat a job I have made of this." If Mr. James had taken one short step further in advance, and learned the last secret of true art, to conceal art, his short stories would have arrived at perfection.

IV.

WHATEVER he may come to be, Mr. James is at present the acknowledged coryphæus of the Ameri-

can school of realists.   A disciple of Balzac, in his
books we leave "the realms of gold" in which the
romancer travels, and come down to the plane of
solid commonplace, —

> "Where the Rudyards cease from Kipling,
> And the Haggards ride no more."

But he is also a disciple of Sainte-Beuve, and is
able to give a well-reasoned exposition of the faith
that is in him as a novelist, as well as to criticise
His critical   the ideals and appreciate the work of
essays.   others.   In a word, he is a thoroughly
equipped critic, whose refined taste, broad spirit,
generous recognition of all that is good, and skill
in the great art of putting things, make his essays
more instructive and entertaining to many readers
than his fiction.   Anybody who has a particle of
literary curiosity, or any appreciation of the graces
of style, may be safely challenged to take up his
"Partial Portraits," or his "French Poets and
Novelists," or his volume on Hawthorne in the
"English Men of Letters" series, and lay the book
down before he has read substantially all of it.   It
is one of the cases where if you say A you must say
B, and so on down the alphabet; to read one page
of the essay on Alfred de Musset, for example,
means that the whole book must be finished out of
hand.   Not that this essay is so pre-eminently good,
— the same result precisely would follow if the
reader opened the book at random; he would be

fascinated, and could not stop except by an effort of will that he would not care to make.

These critical writings throw an illuminating side-light upon the novels of Mr. James, inasmuch as they contain the theory on which his practice of the art of fiction is founded. The *raison d'être* of the novel, he tells us, is that it may represent life, not a part of life merely, but all life. Other than this it has no justification, no place in literature. Obviously, if this principle be fully admitted, it follows that the novelist cannot be restricted in his choice of subjects; he An illuminating side-light. must be permitted to take his own wherever he finds it. He must, indeed, select, but art is a selection that is inclusive; therefore the artist must not deliberately exclude any part of life from his works. This may be an ideal principle for a work of vast design, like Balzac's " Comédie Humaine," but it is a hard saying for the guidance of a novelist whose scheme is modest and whose ambition is something less than world-embracing.

But the principle seems to have an even worse conclusion enfolded in it, nor does Mr. James lack the courage to draw this conclusion. This is, that the art of fiction has nothing to do with morality. If it is true to its aim, if it faithfully tries to represent life, a novel is not to be called either moral or immoral. There are bad novels and good novels, it is true, just as there are good pictures and bad, but in either case the adjective connotes artistic, not moral, qualities. A novel is good when it is well written, it is bad if it is ill written, and Mr. James

No morals in art (?). avows that he can see no other distinction. Now one hopes that the American public is ready to admit the truth of this theory of art neither in the case of pictures nor in the case of novels. The sound, healthy sense of the people, uninstructed in art criticism, revolts from the statement that pictures designed to corrupt the morals of youth, pictures that accomplish such corruption, are to be coldly judged as works of art. Novels that have no better purpose than to drag forth to the light and expose to the gaze of the innocent and pure a mass of festering and putrid moral corruption, cannot be admitted to be good, because of any technical skill shown in the work. The eternal distinction between good and evil, between virtue and vice, cannot be obscured by *dilettante* theories of art.

Mr. James is, to be sure, entitled to the praise of omitting to follow up his own theory to its legitimate conclusions. Some saving grace of commonsense, some unacknowledged remnant of an Anglo-Saxon conscience, has held him back from the

Lacks the courage of his theories. commission of many things that he defends as legitimate. Doubtless he has a desire to be read, and that not as most people read Zola, — in a corner, and with a shamefaced air, — but openly and with a good conscience. No man of American or English birth, unless his mind is hopelessly besmirched, can read a certain type of French novel without apologizing to himself for the insult, and trying to conceal from others what he has done. At worst, he will attempt a lame self-justification on the ground that "so much is said about the book, you know, that I felt I must read it and judge for myself." If he brings such books into his house, he puts them on some shelf of his bookcase where they are hidden by other volumes, carefully locks the doors, and keeps the key in his pocket night and day. If he runs the risk of moral contagion himself, as he might risk catching small-pox or typhus, he has no idea of exposing his wife and children to contamination. The general existence of such a feeling is the strongest evidence that morals cannot really be dissociated from art. Even in France the young girl is most strictly and sedulously kept from seeing pictures or reading books that are constantly before her elders. Why? Whoso can, let him give a reason consistent with the theory that art is unmoral.

V.

BEFORE we can take leave of Mr. James one or two other matters demand at least a passing mention. He not only ranks, by general suffrage, among the first of living novelists and critics, but he has of late become a successful playwright. Some years ago he dramatized his "Daisy Miller," and it had a fair success.   Later his clever stage version His dramatic work. of "The American" won him greater plaudits still, both in London and in the United States.   In London he contended with the disadvantage of a temporary spasm of social feeling against all persons and things American, and won a hearing in spite of this prejudice, which is described by competent observers as unusually bitter.   There has been a recent interesting announcement that Mr. James has written another play, not a dramatization of a previously printed novel, but a wholly new composition.   It has not yet been produced, and any opinion of it can be based only on imagination.

It is remarkable that so few of our American writers have attempted dramatic composition.   To Few American dramatists. one who is not restrained by conscientious scruples play-writing offers great inducements.   No other form of literary work is so well rewarded.   The author of a fifth-rate play, beneath notice for its literary quality, provided it has the "drawing" power, and can hold its place on the stage, receives in the way of royalty as many hundreds a week as the author of a first-rate novel receives thousands in a year.   It may be that American writers are restrained by conscientious scruples; that while they do not see any more moral evil in the drama than in the novel, they do see more moral evil in the theatre than in the

bookstore. Be this as it may, the dramatic successes of American authors may be counted on the
fingers of one hand, with perhaps a finger or two to
spare. This does not necessarily imply, however,
that the exceptional success of Mr. James argues
any high literary value in his plays, for the literary
merit of the modern comedy is surprisingly small.
Such success as he has attained, or may hereafter
attain, by his theatrical ventures, will add more to
his bank account than to his fame.

A word must also be said of the style of Mr.
James. It would not, perhaps, be called a brilliant
style; it lacks the glitter and glow of A gentlemanly
Macaulay as much as the fulminant cor- style.
uscations of Carlyle, but on the other hand it is
not tamely correct. Without absolute lapse into
solecism, a sentence will often have a familiar col-
loquial turn, even in the more serious writings, that
puts the reader at his ease and promotes an excellent understanding between him and the author. It
is the style of the most finished urbanity, of the
broadest and most generous culture; marked by
limpid clearness, by well-bred ease, by flexibility
and variety, not at all by mannerisms. Matthew
Arnold at his best, when he forgot to be elaborately
condescending and offensively ironical, may be
named as perhaps the closest analogue to Mr.
James in the matter of style; only there was about
the Englishman, even when at his best, a certain
stiffness of manner and a lack of nimbleness of

wit, that one does not find in the American.   Mr.
James's study of French literature has had the
happiest effect on his style.   "Whatever is not
clear is not French" is a maxim generally accepted
in France, and if the rule might be reversed, one
would be compelled to pronounce Mr. James more
French than English.

V.

CHARLES DUDLEY WARNER.

VIRGINIA, once known as the mother of states-
men, has of late years yielded her function to
Ohio, but no State has yet wrested from Massachusetts her crown as the mother of poets, orators,
and romancers. The rocky soil and stern climate
of New England, though surpassed by the genial
prairies and rich bottom-lands of West and South
in producing corn and cotton, are unequalled for
producing men. In the culture of the Massachusetts,
fruits of learning and the flowers of rheto- mother of men.
ric, warmer climes and soils more fertile compete
with her in vain. Plain living and high thinking are
still found in Yankeedom oftener than elsewhere,
though in these degenerate days it must be confessed that "plain living" is a figure of speech,
which, translated into every-day language, means
the best of everything and plenty of it. The intellectual supremacy of New England is not wholly
tradition. Perhaps the sceptre is about to depart
to the Middle West, — so we are often informed, with
a triumphant assurance that almost, though not quite,
inspires conviction, — but not until a new generation

of writers gains the ear and heart of the nation, and those to whom we now listen heedfully have gone over to the silent majority.

I.

CHARLES DUDLEY WARNER was born in Massachusetts, in the town of Plainfield, in the year 1829. He came of good though not distinguished Puritan stock. His father, a man of culture, died when he was but five years old. If his son did not fall heir to a large estate, he did inherit a love of literature, though for a time there was little to encourage its growth. Books were not numerous in those days in a New-England family, and what few there were seldom went beyond commentaries, biographies of eminent divines, and theological treatises of the straitest Calvinistic type. We may be certain that young Warner made the best use of what scant opportunities of reading fell in his way. It was not a dreary boyhood that he spent, if we may judge from his " Being a Boy." In this book he has given us a sort of autobiography, less complete than that of Mr. Howells, and not quite so vivid a reproduction of boy life. It is, no doubt, to many a more enjoyable book, on account of its pleasant touches of humor; and it faithfully describes some phases of life in New-England fifty years ago that are now quite non-existent.

Bred among the Puritans.

Young Warner must have been a good student, and he apparently enjoyed rather exceptional advantages for a New-England boy, for he was graduated from Hamilton College in 1851, first His college prizeman in English. He had begun to career. write for " Knickerbocker's " and " Putnam's " magazines while still a college student, and seemed thus predestined to a literary career, but for some years led a rather roving existence, and tried his hand at several occupations. He was in 1853 a member of a surveyor's party on the Missouri frontier; in 1854 he became a student of law at the University of Pennsylvania, being graduated in 1856; and until 1860 he practised law at Chicago. In that year he met his fate, in the shape of an engagement as assistant editor of the Hartford " Press," becoming editor-in-chief the following year. In 1867 this paper was consolidated with the Hartford " Courant," of which Mr. Warner became co-editor with Joseph R. Hawley, — a position which he has held ever since. Becomes a Every day during these years he has journalist. walked to his office — save the times of infrequent absence on vacation — and his daily editorial task has been performed with faithfulness and ability. His literary work has been done in his spare moments, without interference with his regular professional duties; and yet he has accomplished an amount of writing that would make a very creditable record for most professed men of letters. Besides his contributions to the magazines, and his

occasional articles that have never been collected,
he has published since 1870 a good dozen and a
half of volumes, all of which are established favorites
with the public and have a steady sale. His connection in recent years with " Harper's Magazine " is too
well known to need comment. It is enough to say
that on the death of George William Curtis the one
name that suggested itself to every reader as the
name of him who was alone fitted by culture and
traditions to take up the work then laid down, was
Mr. Warner's. And though the "Easy Chair " has
been abolished in name, it still lives in spirit under
Mr. Warner's direction as one of the choicest features of the magazine.

II.

MR. WARNER's connection with literature grew
out of his work as a journalist. In 1868–69 he took
a well-earned holiday abroad, and (as the manner of
editors is) wrote to his journal a series of letters
about what he saw and heard. He had seen rather

First trip
abroad.
more of his own country than is usual with
Americans who go abroad for the first
time ; he had gained a very considerable personal
acquaintance with men and affairs ; he was tolerably
familiar with the history and literature of Europe, —
in short, he was a decidedly intelligent, wide-awake
and observant traveller, and was besides blessed with
a sense of humor. These letters of his had a fresh-

ness, a piquancy, a charm, that speedily gained for the writer a local literary reputation, which did not long remain merely local. As the letters appeared, they were generally copied by the news- papers, and when, several years later, they were republished in a volume with the appropriate title of " Saunterings," a wider circle of readers gave them a welcome rather unusual in the case of such a book.

Saunterings.

These letters, however, while very successful, did not make a " hit." That was accomplished, before the appearance of " Saunterings," by a series of weekly papers on gardening published one summer in the Hartford " Courant." The author's idea seems to have been suggested to him by Horace Greeley's " What I Know about Farming," and he apparently began with some hazy idea of writing a mild bur- lesque on this book. Like the creator of the immortal Pickwick, however, he had not progressed far before his serial took on a char- acter of its own, and totally refused to be finished on the lines he had planned. A good many readers of this article will doubtless recall with a smile the first delightful reading of " My Summer in a Garden " (1870), with its playful wit, its profound moral " ob- servations," its wholesome sentiment, and its whim- sical side-glances at literature, politics, and religion. Mr. Warner's reputation as a humorist was estab- lished by this volume, and confirmed by his " Back- log Studies," which followed two years later. He

My Summer in a Garden.

well deserved his reputation, and has admirably sustained it since. His humor is of the delicate and refined type, not the "side-splitting" sort that it is the fashion to associate with the ádjective American.

Delicacy of humor.   It recalls the traditions of Addison and Steele, and Lamb, and Washington Irving, — not he of the Diedrich Knickerbocker period, but the Irving of the "Sketch Book."

Mr. Warner's reputation as a humorist, as has been said, was established by his papers on gardening, — too well established, shall we say? No doubt his friends considered the success of "My Summer in a Garden" a very fortunate circumstance, and so, from some points of view, it certainly was. One

A dangerous reputation.   might plausibly maintain, from another point of view, that so great a success was on the whole a misfortune. It is a dangerous thing for an author to establish at the outset a reputation as a humorist. To be known as a joker is to risk being known as nothing else. The American public, always ready to cry *encore* to anybody that entertains it, is especially quick to demand the reappearance of one who has made it laugh. We do dearly love to be tickled, we Americans. When the joker of established reputation faces us, we are on a broad grin before he has uttered a word, and we resent it as a personal insult if he fails to justify our expectations by setting us off into fits of laughter. Rarely indeed do we consent to take a man seriously who begins by making us laugh. We apply to him the

Roman theory of the indelibility of orders, — once a humorist always a humorist, we demand shall be his rule of life. Any effort on a humorous writer's part to be instructive, to plead a case seriously, to take a sober view of the world, we resent as in some sort a breach of trust, an attempt to obtain goods under false pretences. He has chosen his character, and, with stern virtue, we insist that he shall live up to it.

There is, perhaps, no better proof of Mr. Warner's power than that he has compelled the unwilling world to take him seriously, in spite of the fact that he made his first hit as a joker. But he has cer- Not a mere tainly not done this without strenuous joker. effort; the very rarity of the achievement is proof not to be controverted of its difficulty. Dr. Holmes tells us, in his pleasant verses on " The Height of the Ridiculous," how dangerous to others it is for a witty writer to be " as funny as he can." It may be dangerous to others, but it is absolutely fatal to himself, unless he has had the prudence previously to establish a reputation for sobriety. Dr. Holmes took the precaution of printing certain hard and dry technical medical works, and thereby making himself highly respected in his professional circle, before he indulged himself in the luxury of making the world laugh. John G. Saxe neglected this precaution, and it was a grief carried with him to the grave that the public would never look on him as anything but a writer of clever parodies and side-splitting jokes in verse. In his later years, Henry W. Shaw was a proverbial philosopher of extraordinary merit; his pithy sentences are the quintessence of practical wisdom, often startling us by the light they flash into the very heart of things; but public opinion compelled him to misspell his shrewd sayings, as the illiterate "Josh Billings," in order to get a

A horrible example. hearing. Mr. Samuel L. Clemens has pub-lished certain books in serious literature, without in the least persuading the public to take him seriously. Many read "The Prince and the Pauper" through with misgiving, lest a huge jest might after all be concealed beneath the apparently sober tale. They failed to enjoy the story, because they were continually and nervously looking for some hidden snare. It is only when, as "Mark Twain," he writes some such trash as "The Adventures of Huckleberry Finn" that this really capable writer can make sure of an appreciative hearing. But Mr. Warner has fairly conquered for himself a place among the solid writers of his day, though he has never scrupled to be funny, even as funny as he can, whenever he has cared to do so. This fact gives him a unique place among American men of letters, and testifies to the possession of mental and moral powers quite unusual. Even so great men as Dean Swift and Sydney Smith found that it is perilous to

A unique place. a man to gain a reputation for wit. Their careers were marred by men's refusal to give credit for solid ability and sterling worth to those on whom it has come to depend for its amusement. One might hesitate, perhaps, to say that Mr. Warner's will eventually be a greater name in letters than these, but he has certainly done what they signally failed to do.

III.

No English authors are more generally read, or are more likely to retain their hold on popular taste, than the essayists. Bacon and Addison and Johnson, Lamb and De Quincey and Macaulay, are names that represent very diverse styles of writ- Popularity of ing, as well as hostile opinions on almost the Essay. every question of religion, history, and politics. Nevertheless, in letters they meet on common ground and have certain common characteristics. If there may be assumed to exist an American school of essayists at all comparable to the English, Mr. Warner must certainly be given a very high place in it, by the suffrages of future readers as well as by the unanimous consent of his own day. The essay seems to be his natural vehicle of thought, the form in which his idea always expresses itself when he does not consciously seek for some other style of expression. This is evidently the case even when his books are not avowedly essays. His books of travel, for instance, are really essays on what he has seen. He is not so much the narrator of the small adventures that befall the modern globe-trotter, or the describer of landscape or of the panorama of town life, as the philosophic observer. The interest of his

Warner essentially an essayist.

books depends far less on the intrinsic interest of what he saw than on how these sights impressed him. He is one of the most subjective of travellers, and one reads " Baddeck " or " On the Nile," not to learn anything about these localities, — one would go to a guidebook or a gazetteer for bald information, — but to enjoy the sensation of looking at them through Mr. Warner's spectacles.

In his avowed essays, Mr. Warner's most ambitious work has, perhaps, been his study of Washington Irving. This first appeared in 1880 as a Preface to the " Geoffrey Crayon edition " of Irving's works, the publication of which was begun in that year by the Messrs. Putnam. The year following, this study, much expanded in details but written on the same general lines, appeared as a volume in the " American Men of Letters " series, of which Mr. Warner is the

Warner and Irving.

general editor. This was a peculiarly congenial task, since there is an evident likeness of character and literary taste between subject and critic. This likeness does not go beyond a general sympathy of method and style; it does not in the least imply imitation. Mr. Warner does not appear to have " formed himself " upon any model, and no mousing critic will ever be able to establish an undue resemblance between his work and that of any other writer; but there are certain elements in Irving's work that are found also in his. He has the more correct taste, according to present standards, especially in that he is more robust and virile, less given to sentimentality, and not so prone to value gentility above manhood. In appreciation of Irving's best work, in gentle but unsparing comment on his unworthy performance, and in the accuracy with which it distinguishes the one from the other, this critical essay must be pronounced work of a very high order.

As has already been intimated, one of Mr. Warner's chief merits as an essayist is his originality. His books are evidently the work of a man who is accustomed to associate with the best people, both in society and in books, but he makes no more parade of his literary than of his *Originality.* social acquaintance. Very entertaining essays have been written, and such will doubtless be written again, that are a mere cento of fine passages openly or secretly borrowed from other writers. One need not deny that such essays have their place, and even show a good deal of cleverness in the writer, if one yet expresses a modest preference for those that do not point out the author as one who has been to a great feast of languages and stolen the scraps, or designate him as an adroit snapper up of unconsidered literary trifles. Mr. Warner does not appear before the world as a critic of literature and of life deep versed in books and shallow in himself. He has doubtless read widely — that appears in a general tone and

7

manner of culture rather than in any vain show of
learning — but he has observed keenly and thought
much, viewing life from many points, looking upon it
with the knowledge of a practical man of affairs, yet
with the mental aloofness of a humorist.

Another great merit of Mr. Warner as an essayist
is his independence. He does not judge according to
conventional standards, but according to the higher
verities of character. This power to see things as they
are, undistorted by the media of current ideas, he
showed in a truly remarkable way in his book "On
Independence. Horseback through the South." The
reader of that book must remember that
its author was in his youth an abolitionist, and throughout his manhood had been a Republican ; that he had
been for many years editor of the chief Republican
newspaper of a State in which almost every citizen
of wealth or culture or social standing was a Republican. There was every reason in the world why he
should have been swayed by ancient prejudices, by
present partisanship, by social feeling, and all unconsciously to himself should have been unable to see
any good in the South, or any prophecy of hope for
the future of that section. Just the reverse was the
fact. Casting aside all the sentiments and prepossessions of his past, Mr. Warner travelled with a mind
open to receive his impressions from the facts themselves, as he saw them. He was not such a fool as
to suppose that he saw in this brief trip everything to
be seen; but what can any traveller do more than

carefully observe and truthfully tell what he does see? This Mr. Warner did with so much intelligence, accuracy, and faithfulness as to win the sturdy dislike of many with whom he had been politically On Horseback associated for years. No Southern man south. could have given a more hopeful picture of the New South, and no Southern man's description would have been received with such credence as was Mr. Warner's. Recognizing the fact that the picture was only a partial one, the people of the North saw in it much to warrant bright hopes of the future, and many of the misapprehensions and misgivings industriously fostered by politicians for selfish purposes were incontinently swept away with other rubbish that had accumulated since the Civil War. Mr. Warner has written books that will probably be read long after this, but nothing that he has ever done constitutes a better title to the grateful remembrance of Americans who love their country.

IV.

EVERY woman, it has been said, has it in her to write at least one novel, but why not every man as well? It was to be expected that so enterprising and successful a writer as Mr. Warner would sooner or later try his hand at fiction ; the only wonder is that he has never yielded to the temptation to " drop into poetry." It is only within a few years, however, that he has made the venture, and his stories are still but two: "Their Pilgrimage," and "A Little Journey in the World." Both of these ventures have been fairly successful,— sufficiently so to warrant **Two novels.** further attempts, but by no means so strikingly successful as to eclipse, or even to rival, his work as an essayist. A disciple of the new school of realism might object that Mr. Warner has not emancipated himself from slavery to traditional theories of the novel. For one thing he shows too much desire to construct a plot — even though he is not entirely successful in the attempt — to win praise from this school. Then in his representation of character he is not so stiffly and dryly realistic as it is latterly the fashion to be. His people talk too much like living men and women. He does not trouble himself to affect profound philosophy of life or art, like one who stalks about,—

> "His cogitative faculties immersed
> In cogibundity of cogitation."

In a word, he is in great danger of excommunication from the church of true believers, who hold, as is well known, that a novel must be so vapid or so foul that nobody can read it. This, however, though it make him the scoff of the elect, is not a serious objection to those of us who are not ashamed to be frankly Philistine, and bow down to our ancient idols, Scott and Dumas, Dickens and Thackeray and George Eliot; who have a sneaking fondness for Robert Louis Stevenson and Rider Haggard, and are not even above being entertained by an adventure of Terence Mulvaney's. Indeed, were one to pick a quarrel with Mr. Warner at all on the score of his fiction, it would be on the ground that he has not the full courage of his convictions. He sometimes sacrifices to the god of realism. Thus "Their Pilgrimage" reads in spots as if it had been written to be a guide-book for certain fashionable resorts and afterward made over into a novel. "A Little Journey in the World" is almost too carefully lifelike a study of the "Napoleon of Finance" with whom more than one recent Wall Street transaction has made every reader of newspapers familiar. These are at worst venial faults.

One is compelled to add, nevertheless, that both these books show a lack of that technical skill in the art of fiction which comes from long practice. They are the books of a gifted amateur, rather than of a trained novelist. They would have been excellent as the first ventures in literature of a young man; they are not without promise as the first novels _{Lack technical} of any writer; but they do not reach a _{skill.} level in fiction comparable to their author's eminence, so well won, in another department of literature. It is hard to say whether he would do better to make further experiment, with a prospect of genuine success before him, or continue to do the work for which he had before shown so singular fitness. The latter course might be pronounced the more prudent, but the former if crowned with success in the end might do more to enhance his repute, enlarge his audience, and increase his usefulness. All depends on whether he

is himself conscious of having a further message for
the world that can be delivered in no other way so
well as through the medium of the novel. It would
be unfortunate if one who stands in the front rank of
essayists should decline to the third rank among
novelists. And yet analogy seems to point out such
a fate as only too probable. Bayard Taylor and
Oliver Wendell Holmes are examples of men who
have done work of the highest worth in poetry and in
general prose writing, but came far short of success
as writers of fiction. Taylor's " Story of Kennett "
and the Autocrat's "Elsie Venner" are far from
failures, they would indeed have been successes for
other men, but they are not worthy of the best powers
of the authors, as shown in other forms of literary
expression. Fiction was not, for either of these, the
best way of giving his message to the world.

Mr. Warner is still in the prime of life. Not for
another decade at least will he need to say, —

> " It is time to be old,
> To take in sail."

In this matter we Americans are improving, and no
longer look on a man as beginning to fall into his
dotage the minute he has passed fifty. The men
between sixty and ninety have, with rare exceptions,
been the real rulers of the world; and when a man of
fifty wins a prominent place in imperial affairs, Englishmen commonly speak of him as rather young for

such responsibility, — this, too, in spite of the fact that Pitt was Premier at twenty-five. That the ripest fruit is yet to come from Mr. Warner's tree of wisdom is a reasonable forecast, which every one who loves his country and enjoys a good book will earnestly hope may be realized.

VI.

THOMAS BAILEY ALDRICH.

A NEW HAMPSHIRE town was a good place to be born and bred in some fifty years ago. Especially if it were a thriving seaport town, with a good "academy" and plenty of chance for fishing and boating, it was a very paradise for a boy. It was such a town — namely, Portsmouth

Portsmouth.

— into which Thomas Bailey Aldrich came November 11, 1836, and it was here that the foundations of his character were laid. Shortly after his birth, his father removed to Louisiana, and there invested his capital in a banking business, — invested it so securely, so the son informs us, that he was never able to get any of it out again. After a few years the father and mother decided that New Orleans was no place for the up-bringing of a Yankee youth, and accordingly "Tom Bailey" was sent back to Portsmouth to sojourn with his relatives and get an education. The history of those years at Portsmouth he has himself given us in "The Story of a Bad Boy" (Boston, 1869), — a book that delights young and old in almost equal measure. The boys enjoy it because it is so per-

fect a picture of a boy's life, full of amusing pranks
and adventures, and written in a spirit of boyish-
ness that manhood had not outgrown. Their elders
value the book somewhat for this very freshness of
spirit, but still more for its delicate humor and the
literary charm of the narrative. "Tom Bailey"
was a bad boy only in a Pickwickian sense. He
was the opposite of the "good little boy" of the
story books, who always died young. That is to
say, he was a genuine boy, who would much rather
spend his stray pennies for "bull's-eyes" The "bad
than give them to send missionaries to boy."
the heathen ; who dearly loved a frolic and had no
desire to be an angel. Of course he got into
scrapes, and of course he tried to run away to
sea, — no New England boy of any spirit failed to do
that at some time, — but these are the worst things
that he brings forward to justify his self-imposed
title. In all of Mr. Aldrich's writings one seems
to detect the savor of that New England boyhood.

I.

THIS happy youth-time and an education that was
to end with a course at Harvard were brought to
an untimely close by the failure of the An interrupted
father's New Orleans business, closely education.
followed by his death. Relatives were ready and
more than willing to furnish the means for the
college course, but young Aldrich, while no dul-

lard at his books, had never developed any marked
scholastic tastes, and he was too self-reliant to accept
the proffered aid.   It seemed better to him to make
the plunge at once into the great world and seek
his fortune.   An uncle who was a merchant in New
York offered him a clerkship, and the youth of six-
teen entered on a business career that he doubtless
hoped would be brilliant, but which proved remarkable for little else than its brevity.

It does not appear, at least from any of his own
confidences, that Mr. Aldrich was a precocious
writer.   He never lisped in verses; he did not
produce plays and novels by the ream in his salad
days; he was too healthy and active a boy to spend
hours sacred to play in spoiling paper and inking
himself.   But he had the root of the matter in him
Drops into   none the less, and early in his "teens"
Poetry.   his bent showed itself. · The "Ballad of
Babie Bell" he had written and printed before he
was twenty; and if he has written stronger verses
since, he has not written anything more sweet and
tenderly pathetic.   One may gratefully note in
passing, as a mark of sounder taste, that in the
later editions of his poems Mr. Aldrich has dropped
the affected spelling that originally spoiled this
poem, and we have now the "Ballad of Baby Bell."
It was a few affectations like this, and a somewhat
dandified style of portrait published with some of
his earlier works, that made many people look on
Mr. Aldrich for a long time as a literary Miss

Nancy. They were slow in giving him credit for
the real virile power that his writings show.

Even during his clerkship days Mr. Aldrich spent
more hours at the shrine of the Muses than in the
temple of Mammon. This is not to say that he
was an idle and inefficient clerk; it is merely to
say that his business service, though conscientious,
was perfunctory, and that the work to which his
heart was given was that of letters. Nor need
one hesitate to say that he chose the better part.
Doubtless the posting of ledgers is a calling as full
of dignity and as worthy of honor as that of poet
or romancer, provided one has the vocation and
honestly obeys it.

> " Who sweeps a room as for Thy cause
> Makes that and th' action fine."

But the posting of ledgers is not honorable work
for him who is conscious of another vocation; it
can at best be nothing more than an honest way of
earning his bread. For three years the budding
author continued his attempt to serve two masters,
and then gave up the struggle, devoting The parting of
himself without reserve to the Muses. A the ways.
happy choice this was for American literature, and
a fortunate one it has proved to be for the author,
but the issue was for a time doubtful. At that day
there was little encouragement for a young man
to undertake the earning of a living by his pen.
" Knickerbocker's " and " Putnam's " and " Godey's "

were the only periodicals then published that could accept and pay for even an occasional contribution. Mr. Aldrich was compelled, therefore, to look for some semi-literary occupation that would ensure him a living while he wrote. This he found for a time in a publishing house, for which he acted as "reader" of manuscripts submitted for publication, and as a proof-reader also. In 1856 he joined the staff of the "Home Journal," then conducted by Messrs. Willis and Morris.

Mr. Aldrich's connection with New York lasted, with varying fortunes, until 1870. While here he cemented friendships with many of the young men

Early friendships. of letters of his day, — notably with Stedman, Stoddard, and Bayard Taylor, — friendships that have lasted unbroken to the present day, or have been severed only by death. He seems to have been a man who made friends easily, and he had also the qualities that hold friends once made. How much he is respected and admired by his fellow-craftsmen was shown clearly in the public dinner lately given him by New York men of letters, who vied with one another to do him fitting honor. But aside from this circle of friends, it would be hard to say that the New York experiences of Mr. Aldrich made any impression on his life and work, — any impression that can be identified, one means, of course. That these years had an important part in the making of the man it would be absurd to question. The point is that in his writings there is singularly little trace of his New York life. He has attempted no study of metropolitan life in his more ambitious work, and even in his short stories and *jeux d'esprit* the tone of the metropolis is not discernible. One might almost infer that he has, for some reason good in his own sight, deliberately avoided turning his New York life to account in his verse and fiction. His readers may well regret that this is the case, for he is a man in some ways peculiarly fitted both to appreciate and to describe life in New York.

II.

THE second period in Mr. Aldrich's literary career began with his removal to Boston, in 1870, to become the editor of "Every Satur- A journalistic day," a young and ambitious periodical, experiment. that it was hoped would become a sort of American "Spectator." More purely literary than the "Nation," it was not adapted to interest and hold so large a constituency of readers, and its success did not meet the expectations of the founders. It may be doubted whether a high-class literary weekly can succeed in the United States,— the "Critic" is the nearest approach to such a paper, — but it seems clear that the failure of "Every Saturday" to be a brilliant success was, at any rate, no fault of its editor. A better choice for the post could not well

have been made. He had published "The Dells,"
a volume of verse, in 1855; "Babie Bell and Other
Poems " in 1856; and collected editions of his
poems in 1863 and 1865 respectively. He had
experience in practical work for periodicals and
publishers that had prepared him for editing such
a journal with intelligent appreciation of the public
taste, and then he had a considerable personal acquaintance with American writers that was of great
value to a young periodical, since it was easy for
him to secure the co-operation of the best talent.
All this did not avail, however, to make the paper
financially successful. When in 1874 its publication was suspended, Mr. Aldrich might have made
his valedictory in Cato's words : —

> " 'T is not in mortals to command success,
>   But we 'll do more, Sempronius ; we 'll deserve it."

This did not complete his editorial career.   A
few years later — in 1881, to be precise — Mr.
Editor of the   Howells retired from the editorship of
Atlantic.   "The Atlantic Monthly," and the publishers naturally turned to Mr. Aldrich as to a fore-
ordained successor.   For some years he had been
a regular and welcome contributor to the magazine;
he was familiar with its traditions, and by training
and temperament was suited to carry on the work,
with some infusion of original ideas, but avoiding
any marked break with the past.   This work he
continued until 1890.   Without disparagement of

other editors the "Atlantic" has had — and there has been a brilliant succession of them — one can not fail to recognize in the work of these years the very highest editorial and literary ability. "A nightingale dies for shame if another bird sings better," says some old writer, but Mr. Aldrich has never shown such jealousy of his fellow-singers. On the contrary, it was his good fortune to bring before the public for the first time writers, in both verse and prose, of now established reputation; and others, who may have appeared in print before, made their present fame during his editorship. Among these it suffices to mention as examples "Charles Egbert Craddock" (Miss Murfree), Sarah Orne Jewett, and Louise Imogen Guiney, with the addition, possibly, of Arthur Sherburne Hardy, — though his reputation was fairly made, in the first instance, by the publication of a story Authors dis-
that had not appeared serially. It was covered.
creditable to the editor's enterprise, however, that he promptly "annexed" the new writer. Mr. Aldrich held most of the regular staff of "Atlantic" writers, even in the face of hot competition from New York magazines, and their offers of higher prices for work. Authors are but human, however, and it is not wonderful that some forsook their New England divinity and went after strange gods.

Since going to Boston, Mr Aldrich's most impor-
tant publications have been : two new and enlarged editions of his poems (in 1873 and 1876), "Mar-

jorie Daw and Other Stories " (1873), " Prudence
Palfrey" (1874), "The Queen of Sheba" (1877),
His books. "The Stillwater Tragedy " (1880), " From
Ponkapog to Pesth," and "Mercedes"
(both 1883). All the volumes named, save the last,
are prose. The title-work of the last volume is a
prose tragedy, but at least half the book consists of
"Later Lyrics." This is a very respectable list of
works, as regards number merely, and if it does
not entitle the author to be reckoned the peer of
Messrs. Howells and Crawford in industry, it shows
that he has by no means idled his time aimlessly
away.

III.

MR. ALDRICH'S prose writings fully deserve their
vogue. There are no cleverer short stories than
"Marjorie Daw" and its companions. Marjorie in
The prose
writings. particular is a masterpiece, the surprising
conclusion being artfully concealed from
the reader until the very last sentence. The only
story with which it can be fairly compared, in this
particular, is Mr. Frank R. Stockton's "The Lady
or the Tiger?" The dénouement of Mr. Stockton's
story may be pronounced the more humorous, but
that of Mr. Aldrich's is certainly the more witty.
And in the matter of style, Mr. Stockton is nowhere
in comparison with Mr. Aldrich. There is in the
latter's prose a *bonhomie*, — we have no adequate

English phrase for this combination of high spirits and gentlemanly manner,—a deftness of touch, a sureness of aim, a piquancy of flavor, a playfulness of wit, a delicacy of humor, that make it perfectly delightful reading. No other of our writers has caught so much of the spirit of French prose, save Mr. Henry James; and Mr. Aldrich deserves the praise that, while he has learned from the French all that they have to teach, he has still remained essentially American.

We have been considering his short stories only thus far, but what has been said is true of the other fictions. Indeed, with the single excep- Long short- tion of "The Stillwater Tragedy," these stories. books are nothing else than long short-stories, if such a Hibernicism be permissible. "The Queen of Sheba" requires very large type and very thick "leads" to draw it out into the decent semblance of a duodecimo novel, and "Prudence Palfrey" is little better. But this is a trifling detail after all; what classifies these books with short stories is not their actual length, but quality of plot. In neither of the two volumes named is there material for a novel. The stories are so essentially simple and uncomplicated, the characters are so few and so easily developed, that to spin these yarns out to the orthodox novel limit would be to dilute all the flavor and sparkle into unmitigated flatness. Mr. Aldrich has too nice a taste to spoil good wine by adding three times its bulk of water; he is too good

8

an artist to disregard the self-limited development of his plot.

In "The Stillwater Tragedy" he has a subject that justifies, if it does not require, more elaborate treatment. His characters are more complex; his plot demands space for working out to a natural conclusion; his situations are dramatic. It is, therefore, his most ambitious prose work, and it shows more power than anything else he has written. This is true of the artistic treatment of the theme only; the moral element in the book, while wholesome in intent, is vitiated by sentiment. There **The labor** has been no treatment of the vexed **question.** "labor question" in fiction that is not weakened by its sentimental tone. Sympathy with one side or the other has prevented all novelists from throwing the white light of truth on the subject, and it is probably in the nature of things that this should always be the case. Mr. Aldrich comes short of the highest achievement precisely where Dickens and Charles Reade had failed before him, and it must therefore be allowed that he has at least failed in good company. The excellences of the story are quite independent of this defect, and the book was so good as to warrant the hope that its author would at the next trial rise much higher. In the dozen years that have since passed there has been no next trial, and this book therefore remains his high-water mark in prose writing.

IV.

As a poet, Mr. Aldrich deserves more general recognition than he has ever received. "The Ballad of Baby Bell," one of his earliest poems, still remains that by which he is chiefly known to the majority of readers. His circle of admirers is comparatively small, but it comprises all who have a genuine love for poetry, and a cultivated taste, — all who can enjoy

His verse.

> "A perpetual feast of nectar'd sweets,
> Where no crude surfeit reigns."

We have among our American poets, living and dead, no more intelligent and conscientious artist in verse. His conception of the poet's art is well expressed in some lines to an unnamed author: —

> "Great thoughts in crude, inadequate verse set forth,
> Lose half their preciousness, and ever must.
> Unless the diamond with its own rich dust
> Be cut and polished, it seems little worth."

There has been no lack of the cutting and polishing in Mr. Aldrich's verse, and his workmanship approaches perfection. He excels in short poems. A poetic thought that can be adequately set forth in a quatrain, a sonnet, a dozen couplets, or a half-dozen stanzas, he treats to perfection, but he has never shown the same ability to handle a large theme. He is a carver of exquisite cameos, not a sculptor of great statues, or a painter

A carver of cameos.

of splendid landscapes. Let it not be supposed that this is said in any spirit of disparagement; it is merely a proper description of the work he has chosen to do. Critics of all time are agreed that the lyrics of Sappho evince a poetic genius not less fine — and perhaps a more precious poetic art — than the epics of Homer. To carve cameos may be an art as dignified and as worthy of the world's honor as the building of cathedrals: that depends on the artist, rather than on the bulk of his product.

The fault of American literature in general is hasty, crude workmanship. Our writers are not sufficiently sincere; they lack genuine reverence for their art; conscientious fidelity in details they have never learned. This is true of even so affluent a genius, so perfect an artist when he chose to take *Defect of* pains, as Lowell; and how much truer it is *American literature.* of the ninety and nine who lack his genius and resemble him only in their faults. American authors consider their work done when it is only well begun, — when they have given a first crude, imperfect expression to a happy inspiration. The weeks and months of patient toil needed to cut and polish the rough gem, they are either unable or unwilling to give. So far as the artistic defects of American literature may be fairly ascribed to inability to do better work, the failure may be pardonable. The slaves of the pen must live of the pen; and bread must be had, if the writing suffers

by undue haste to publish. Poetry, however, is
rather a case apart. In most instances the publication of verses puts little money in their author's
purse, — or in the publisher's either, if all be true
that's said, — and the temptation to market one's
unripe fruit is not great. The inducement being
so small, whether from poverty or from cupidity,
to rush into the market-place out of due time, he
who prints his verse before he has made it as good
as he can is without excuse. Mr. Aldrich has no
cause to enter any plea for mitigation of judgment.
He has certainly done his best, and that is to succeed in the noblest sense, as he himself says in one
of his sugar'd sonnets : —

> " Enamoured architect of airy rhyme,
>   Build as thou wilt; heed not what each man says.
>   Good souls, but innocent of dreamers' ways,
>   Will come, and marvel why thou wastest time ;
>   Others, beholding how thy turrets climb
>   'Twixt theirs and heaven, will hate thee all their days;
>   But most beware of those who come to praise.
>   O Wondersmith, O worker in sublime
>   And heaven-sent dreams, let art be all in all;
>   Build as thou wilt, unspoiled by praise or blame,
>   Build as thou wilt, and as thy light is given :
>   Then, if at last the airy structure fall,
>   Dissolve, and vanish — take thyself no shame.
>   They fail, and they alone, who have not striven."

It cannot be said, because Mr. Aldrich has confined himself chiefly to "short swallow-flights of
song," that he is incapable of a longer effort. His

"Spring in New England" is the best ode that
Decoration Day has inspired, though not the best
known; and the longest of his poems, "Judith," is
conceived in the spirit of Milton and composed in
the spirit of Keats.   One suggests these two names
only to characterize the work, not to imply doubt of
its original power.   Probably Mr. Aldrich is too
fastidious in taste, too careful in workmanship, to
attempt a long poem, in despair of ever finishing
it according to his high standard of excellence.

In most of his verse there is a blithe and debonair
spirit.   Especially is the humor that flashes from
His wholesome many of the poems marked by this fresh-
spirit. ness of spirit.   Even in the youthful
verses there is singularly little of that cynical,
world-worn manner affected by juvenile poets in
general. Mr. Aldrich has never posed as a Blighted
Being.   The dash of cynicism that one occasionally
lights on is of the quiet sort that a well-bred man
of the world now and then shows, — not a manner
assumed for effect, but a genuine, though a passing,
mood.   If one describe the poems as a whole, in
any terms but those of praise, it is only to express
some surprise mingled with regret that the author
has not more frequently struck a note that thrills
one's higher nature.   Yet his art is so fine at its
best, so apparently spontaneous in its finished
excellence, that all regret vanishes as one reads.
What, for instance, could be finer than this closing
stanza from "Spring in New England?" —

> " Hark! 'tis the bluebird's venturous strain
>   High on the old fringed elm at the gate —
>   Sweet-voiced, valiant on the swaying bough,
>   Alert, elate,
>   Dodging the fitful spits of snow,
>   New-England's poet-laureate
> Telling us Spring has come again!"

Verse like that ranks alongside of the best of Shelley or Wordsworth; one's sole lament is that there should be so little of it, and that he who is so well qualified to be nature's poet should have employed himself so largely with society verse.

V.

AMERICAN writers who have produced a play that has real literary merit, and is at the same time adapted to stage representation, are few indeed. Mr. Aldrich holds an honorable rank among this small band by reason of his "Mercedes." This drama was published in 1884, but *Mercedes.* it was not acted until 1893, when it held the stage at Palmer's Theatre, New York, for a week. This is a brief, but a decided, dramatic success. Though divided into two acts or scenes, the drama is practically continuous. In the first scene we learn from a dialogue at the bivouac fire that Captain Luvois has been ordered to attack the Spanish hamlet of Arguano with a detachment of French soldiers, and put all the inhabitants to the

sword. The duty is most unwelcome, for in that
village dwells the woman he loves, whom he has
been compelled to leave by the exigencies of military service. He is determined to save her. In
the second act Mercedes is discovered in the
hamlet with her child, unable to flee with her
neighbors because she cannot abandon her old
grandmother. The soldiers find wine, which they
believe has been poisoned. They demand that
Mercedes drink some of it as a test; and, believing
her lover false, and sick of life, she drinks and
gives some of the wine to her child. The soldiers
then drink and all are poisoned. Just then Luvois
arrives, and Mercedes lives only long enough to
hear that he has been faithful and still loves her;
but he, too, has drunk of the wine before seeing
"Supp'd full her. The curtain falls on a stage
with horrors." strewed with corpses. This is tragedy
in allopathic doses, to be sure, yet the incident is
probable, possibly historical, and the strength of its
situations is obvious and undeniable. The theme
is worked out in the details with dignity, self-
restraint, and power, and the literary finish is what
we always expect, and never expect in vain, from
Mr. Aldrich. Altogether, the production of the
play must be pronounced most gratifying, since
it was well staged and well acted, and pleased
about equally the critics and the public. It does
not place the author among the great dramatists,
but it marks him a successful playwright, and war-

rants expectations of something stronger when he next essays dramatic composition.

VI.

IT is the distinction of Mr. Aldrich that he belongs to the small group of American writers who have a European reputation. Several of his stories have received the compliment of publication in a French version in the "Revue des deux Mondes," which is the blue ribbon of the *The British* novelist. His books have been "pirated" *"pirate."* freely by those canny European publishers who have stolen both wisely and too well. His name is sometimes mentioned in English periodicals with that tone of polite condescension which the Briton means for compliment. It is true that the references to him and his writings are not always intelligent, and betray on the writer's part a plentiful lack of all knowledge save the one fact that Mr. Aldrich does exist. Mr. Brander Matthews not long ago, in the course of some strictures on the insularity of English men of letters, instanced the case of a critic of pretensions who had classified the "Queen of Sheba" among the poems of Mr. Aldrich. He very properly said that this was a sort of ignorance that would be considered disgraceful in an American writing of Mr. Andrew Lang, for instance. Mr. Lang came to the defence of his brothers of the craft, and denied their insularity, but in so doing gave an amusing proof that Mr. Matthews was right. "I have not read Mr. Aldrich's 'Queen of Sheba'" (I quote from memory, but with substantial correctness, I am sure), "but I am quite willing to believe that it is equal to his other poems." The point, of course, is Insular ignorance. that the Briton is not compelled to write about American authors, — he always has the privilege of silence, — but if he does undertake to write about them, he should at least be familiar enough with the title-pages of the books mentioned not to confound a prose romance with poetry. Mr. Matthews was quite justified in directing attention to the fact that the English man of letters seldom thinks it worth his while to learn something about American matters before he undertakes to write about them. Why, indeed, should he, since he writes for a public so much more ignorant than himself that his worst errors, and even his deliberate inventions, will pass for accurate knowledge?

Mr. Aldrich is still on the sunny side of sixty. His friends declare that he has discovered the Reserved power. secret of perpetual youth, and that while others grow gray and infirm, he is still "alert, elate," with body unworn and mind unflagging, capable of greater things than he has yet accomplished. There is, as one reads his books, an impression left that he has never quite put forth his full strength. The well-poised mind and deliberate art imply reserve power. That this may prove to be a correct forecast, and that the crowning masterpiece is yet to come, will be hoped by none so devoutly as by those who appreciate most justly both. the excellence and the defect of what Mr. Aldrich has thus far produced.

VII.

MARK TWAIN.

O N a certain street in Hartford, Conn., towns-
men showing the local lions to the visitor
from abroad will point with pride to a group of
three comfortable, not to say handsome, houses as
the homes of as many distinguished American
writers. In one of these houses lives Charles
Three Hart-
ford "lions." Dudley Warner, in another, Harriet
Beecher Stowe; the third, the finest of
the three, is the winter home of the writer known
the world over as Mark Twain. His winter home
only is here, for this favorite of fortune has a
summer home also, at Elmira, N. Y., where he has
done most of his literary work of late years. Mr.
Clemens is not like most American authors; his
fertile season is the hot weather, when brain-
workers in general are either taking a vacation or
envying those who can take one. To a building
detached from the house, and a room accessible to
no one when he has once locked the door, he
repairs every morning after breakfast, and remains
there the better part of the day with his work.
Those who think that books, especially the books

of a "funny man," write themselves will do well not to express that opinion within reach of Mark Twain's arm — or pen. No American writer has won his fame by more honorable toil than Mr. Clemens.

I.

IT is not surprising that Mr. Warner and Mrs. Stowe should be neighbors in a staid Connecticut town; Mrs. Stowe was born in that State, and Mr. Warner is a New Englander. But that Mark Twain should have drifted to Hartford as a permanent residence is only less astonishing than Mr. Cable's emigration from New Orleans to Northampton, Mass. For Samuel Langhorne Clemens first saw the light in the village of Florida, ^{A Missouri boy.} State of Missouri. This was in 1835, at a time when Missouri was on the very frontier of civilization, and its exact limits had not yet been defined. The condition of this western country at that time may be inferred from the fact that St. Louis was then a city of some twelve thousand people, while Chicago was not incorporated as a city until 1837, when it had rather more than four thousand inhabitants. It is not wonderful, therefore, that all the education young Clemens received was what he could obtain in the village school of Hannibal. This was supplemented by his training in a printing-office, which he entered at the age of thirteen.

A bright boy in an old-fashioned printing-office was certain to pick up a very fair education of the practical kind. He would learn spelling, punctuation, and the other minor moralities of literature, as these things are seldom learned by boys whose schooling may have been better, but who enter other callings. He would also gain some knowledge of machinery; for in a country office the boy has to learn to work the press, and to repair it when it gets out of order, as it has a trick of doing often.

When the lad had acquired enough skill to call himself a journeyman printer he set out to see the world, and his native State thenceforth saw little The "jour" of him. Those were the halycon days printer. of the "jour" printer; the world was all before him where to choose. He set out, with no kit of tools to carry, and with certainty of employment almost anywhere he might go, or of assistance from his fellows in the craft, thanks to a sort of free-masonry that prevailed everywhere among them. He might work his passage all around the continent and see life in all its phases, as no man of any other trade or profession could. We are told that Mr. Clemens worked at his trade by turns in St. Louis, Cincinnati, Philadelphia, and New York; and doubtless, if the whole truth were known, this would be a very imperfect catalogue of the places where he has stood at the case in his day.

By 1851 he had tired of wandering about in this way, and became enamoured of another calling not less adventurous. He "learned the river" and became a Mississippi pilot, A Mississippi pilot. continuing in this work for some ten years it would seem. At any rate, the next change in his life of which one can learn is his appointment in 1861 as private secretary to his brother, who had obtained an appointment as Secretary of the Territory of Nevada. Going to Nevada means, sooner or later, going into mining. It seems Tries mining, to have been sooner with Mr. Clemens, but he failed to "make his pile," as the miners say, though he did lay the foundations for the sympathetic studies of life in this region that he gave the world in "Roughing It." No doubt it was this failure that turned him again to the printing-office, but this time he had a promotion; he was made city editor of the Virginia City "Enterprise." The rise from the composing-room to the editorial desk in those days, and in a far western town, was not so long a step. One conjectures that the city editor of the "Enterprise" "surprised by himself" the entire reportorial staff, and usually then journalism. carried his office in his hat. What we are more interested to know than the number of assistants this city editor had is the fact that he began while in this service to write humorous contributions, and to sign them "Mark Twain,"—a reminiscence of his pilot days, when this was a

frequent call from the man who was taking sound
ings from the deck of a Mississippi boat.

Mr. Clemens was now beginning his real work,
but he had not yet settled into his stride, if we may
borrow a phrase from athletics.   In 1865 we find
him in San Francisco, engaging in journalism and
in mining operations.   He spent six months of the
following year in Hawaii, and on his return delivered lectures in California.   These, together with
other of his published writings, were gathered into
The Jumping   a volume called "The Jumping Frog and
Frog.   Other Sketches" (New York, 1867).   He
was now fairly launched in a literary career, but his
first great success was to come, though he had not
long to wait for it.   The publication of his account
of a voyage through the Mediterranean, and travels
Innocents   in the adjoining countries, under the title
Abroad.   of "The Innocents Abroad" (Hartford,
1869), made him famous at once; one hundred and
twenty-five thousand copies were sold in three
years, and probably not less than half a million
copies have been sold by now, and yet the public
is not tired of buying it.   The fortunate author
was now independent.   After a brief connection with
the "Buffalo Express," and the editing of a department in the "Galaxy," he settled for the rest of
his life in Hartford,—not to be idle, but to work
leisurely, with little or no temptation to spoil his
writing by undue haste to get it to market.   Since
then he has published: "Roughing It" (Hartford,

1872), "The Adventures of Tom Sawyer" (Hartford, 1876), "A Tramp Abroad" (Hartford, 1880), "The Prince and the Pauper" (New York, Other books. 1882), "The Adventures of Huckleberry Finn" (New York, 1884), "A Yankee at King Arthur's Court," (New York, 1889), besides several other volumes of less note. He has also edited "A Library of Wit and Humor" (New York, 1888), the best collection ever made of representative pieces by American humorists. In the preface he characteristically remarks that, could he have had his way, the "Library" would have consisted wholly of extracts from his own works. The reader may season this with as many grains of salt as he chooses.

II.

THE immediate and permanent popularity of "Innocents Abroad" is not wonderful; it is a book of even greater merit than the public gave it credit for possessing. It was read and enjoyed for its fun, and though nearly twenty-five years have passed, it is still a funny book, whether one reads it now for the first or the forty-first time. But underneath the fun was an earnest purpose that the great mass of readers failed to see at the time, and even yet imperfectly appreciate. This purpose was to tell, not how an American ought to feel on seeing the sights of the Old World, but how he actually does

feel if he is honest with himself. From time im-
memorial, books of travel had been written

A hater of
shams.
by Americans purporting to record their
experiences, but really telling only what the writers
thought they might, could, would, or should have
experienced. This is a very familiar type of the
genus globe-trotter; specimens of it are seen everywhere in Europe, Murray or Baedeker constantly
in hand and carefully conned, lest they dilate with
the wrong emotion — or, what is almost as bad,
fail to dilate with the proper emotion at the right
instant. For sham sentiment, sham love of art,
sham adventures, Mark Twain had no tolerance,
and he gave these shams no quarter in his book.
"Cervantes smiled Spain's chivalry away" is a fine
phrase of Byron's, which, like most fine phrases,
is not true. What Cervantes did was to "smile
away" the ridiculous romances of chivalry, — chivalry had been long dead in his day, — the impossible tales of knightly adventure, outdoing the
deeds of the doughty Baron Munchausen, that were
produced in shoals by the penny-a-liners of his
time. Not since this feat of Cervantes has a
wholesome burst of merriment cleared the air more
effectually or banished a greater humbug from literature than when "The Innocents Abroad" laughed
away the sentimental, the romantic book of travels.

Mark Twain, perhaps, erred somewhat on the
other side. His bump of reverence must be admitted to be practically non-existent; and while

his jests about the saints may make the unskilful laugh, the judicious grieve. The fact seems to be that he sees so clearly the humbug and pretence and superstition beneath things conventionally held to be sacred that he sometimes fails to see that they are not all sham, and that there is really something sacred there. In truth, Mark Twain has been slow to learn that "quips and cranks and wanton wiles" are not always in good taste. Throughout the book the author was just *A frank Philistine.* a little too hard-headed, too realistic, too unimpressionable, too frankly Philistine, for entire truthfulness and good taste; but it may have seemed necessary to exaggerate something on this side in order to furnish an antidote to mawkish sentimentality. His lesson would have been less effective if it had not been now and then a trifle bitter to the taste. Since that time travellers have actually dared to tell the truth; or shall we say that they have been afraid to scribble lies so recklessly? Whichever way one looks at the matter, there is no doubt that American literature, so far as it has dealt with Europe and things European, has been more natural, wholesome, and self-respecting since the tour of this shrewd Innocent.

The same earnestness of purpose underlies much else that Mark Twain has written, especially "The Prince and the Pauper," and "A Yankee *Two English tales.* at King Arthur's Court." The careless reader no doubt sees nothing in the first of these

books but a capital tale for boys. He cannot help
seeing that, for it is a story of absorbing interest,
accurate in its historical setting, and told in remarkably good English.   In the latter book he will no
doubt discover nothing more than rollicking humor
and a burlesque of "Morte d'Arthur." This is to
see only what lies on the surface of these volumes,
without comprehending their aim, or sympathizing
with the spirit.   Not the old prophet of Chelsea
The seamy side himself was a more inveterate hater of
of chivalry.   sham and cant than Mark Twain.   Much
of the glamour of chivalry is as unreal as the
tinsel splendors of the stage; to study history is
like going behind the scenes of a theatre, a disen-
chantment as thorough as it is speedy.   "Morte
d'Arthur" and Tennyson's "Idylls of the King"
present to the unsophisticated a very beautiful, but
a very shadowy and unsubstantial picture of Britain
thirteen centuries ago.   Even in these romances
a glimpse of the real sordidness and squalor and
poverty of the people may now and then be caught
amid all the pomp and circumstance of chivalry,
and yet nobody has had the pitiless courage heretofore to let the full blaze of the sun into these
regions where the lime-light of fancy has had full
sway, that we might see what the berouged heroes
and heroines actually are.

But Mark Twain has one quality to which Carlyle
never attained; joined to his hatred of shams is a
hearty and genuine love of liberty.   His books could

never have been written by one not born in the
United States.   His love of liberty is characteristic in its manifestation.   In a French-   A lover of
man it would have found vent in essays   liberty.
on the text of *liberté, fraternité, égalité,* but eloquent
writing about abstractions is not the way in which
an American finds voice for his sentiments.   Mark
Twain's love of liberty is shown unostentatiously,
incidentally as it were, in his sympathy for, and
championship of, the down-trodden and oppressed.
He says to us, in effect: "Here you have been
admiring the age of chivalry; this is what your
King Arthur, your spotless Galahad, your valiant
Launcelot made of the common people.   Spending
their lives in the righting of imaginary wrongs,
they were perpetuating with all their energy a system of the most frightful cruelty and oppression.
Cease admiring these heroes, and execrate them as
they deserve."   This, to be sure, is a one-sided
view, but it is one that we need to take in endeavor-
ing to comprehend the England of King Arthur.
There is no danger that we shall overlook the
romantic and picturesque view while Malory and
Tennyson are read, but it is wholesome for us sometimes to feel the weight of misery that oppressed
all beneath the privileged classes in England's days
of chivalry.   No books are better fitted to help a
student of history "orient himself," as the French
phrase it, than these two of Mark Twain's.

III.

EXCEPT in the two books that may be called historic romances, Mark Twain has been a consistent realist.   He was probably as innocent of intent to belong to the realistic school when he **Realism.** began writing as Molière's old gentleman had all his life been of the intent to talk prose.   He was realistic because it "came sort o' nateral" to him, as a Yankee would say.   His first books were the outcome of his personal experiences. These were many and varied, for few men have knocked about the world more, or viewed life from so many points.   Bret Harte has written of life on the Pacific coast with greater appreciation of its romantic and picturesque features, but one suspects with considerably less truthfulness in detail.   The shady heroes and heroines of Bret Harte's tales are of a quality that suggests an amalgam of Byron and Smollett; they smack strongly of Bowery melodrama.   Mark Twain's "Roughing It" is a wholesome book, and as accurate in its details as a photograph, but there is nothing romantic or thrilling about it.

It is in the Mississippi Valley, however, that our author finds himself most at home, not only because his knowledge of it is more comprehensive and minutely accurate, but because it is a more congenial field.   Mark Twain understands California, admires it even, but he loves the great river and the folk who dwell alongside it. He is especially happy in his delineation of the boy of _{Understands} this region. If ever any writer under- _{the boy.} stood boy nature in general, from A to izzard, the name of that writer is Mark Twain. He has explored all its depths and shallows, and in his characters of Tom Sawyer and Huckleberry Finn he has given us such a study of the American boy as will be sought in vain elsewhere. He has done more than this; he has given us a faithful pictuie, painfully realistic in details, of the *ante bellum* social condition of the Mississippi Valley. This realism redeems the books from what would otherwise seem worthlessness, and gives them a positive value.

One ought also to recognize the great merit of this writer's short stories. Most of these stories are humorous in their fundamental conception, or have a vein of humor running through them, but they are not, for the most part, boisterously funny. They range in style from the avowedly _{His short} funny tale of "The Jumping Frog of Cale- _{stories.} veras" to the surface sobriety of "The £1,000,000 Bank Note." In the composition of the short story, Mark Twain is so evidently perfecting his art as to warrant one in hazarding the prediction that much of his best work in future is likely to be done along this line.

IV.

EVEN our English cousins, — as a rule, not too lenient in their judgments of kin across the sea, — admit that American humor has a distinct flavor. Not only so, they also admit that this flavor is delightful. To their tastes there is something wild and gamy about American humor, a tang that is both a new sensation and a continuous source of English appre- enjoyment. British commendation of ciation. American humor, however, is not always as discriminating as it is hearty. We must allow Englishmen the praise of having been prompt to appreciate Artemus Ward the only; but of late years they seem impervious to American humor, except of one type — that which depends for its effect on exaggeration. Exaggeration is, no doubt, one legitimate species of humor. The essence of humor lies in the perception of incongruity, and the effect of incongruity may be produced by exaggeration. This is the more effectively done if the style is dry; the writer must give no sign, until the very end (if even there) that he does not take himself seriously. The narrator must not by a tone of voice or change of facial expression betray any lack of exact veracity in his tale, or the effect is measurably lost. Mark Twain has frequently shown himself to be master of this style of humor. He can invent the most tremendous absurdities, and tell them with such an air of seriousness as must frequently deceive the unwary.

But this is not, as English readers mistakenly imagine, the best type of American humor; it is not even the type in which Mark Twain reaches his highest level. Exaggeration is comparatively cheap humor. Anybody can lie, and the kind of Mark Twain's humor most admired abroad is simply the lie of circumstance minus the intent to deceive. It is morally innocuous, therefore, but it is bad art. No doubt it is frequently successful in provoking laughter, but the quality of humor is not to be gauged by the loudness of the hearers' guffaws. The most delightful fun is that which at most provokes no more than a quiet smile, but is susceptible of repeated enjoyment when the most hilarious joke is received in a grim silence more expressive than words. To borrow a metaphor from science, humor is the electricity of literature, but in its finest manifestation it is not static but dynamic. The permanent charm of humorous writing is generally in inverse ratio to its power to incite boisterous merriment when first read. The joker who at first gives one a pain in the side soon induces "that tired feeling" which is fatal to continued interest. It is Mark Twain's misfortune at present to be appreciated abroad mainly for that which is ephemeral in his writings. His broad humanity, his gift of seeing far below the surface of life, his subtle comprehension

Cheap humor.

of human nature, and his realistic method, are but
dimly apprehended by those Britons who go off in
convulsions of laughter the moment his name is
mentioned. It is probably in vain for us to protest against this misjudgment of American authors
by Britons —

> " Against stupidity the very gods
> Themselves contend in vain."

A false standard of what is truly "American"
has been set up abroad, and only what conforms to
that standard wins admiration. For that reason
British readers have gone wild over Bret Harte and
Joaquin Miller, while they neglected Bryant and
Holmes, and for a time even Lowell, on the ground
that the latter were "really more English than
American, you know." Their own countrymen
have a juster notion of the relative standing of
American authors. In the case of Mark Twain
they do not believe that he is rated too high by
foreign critics and readers, but that his true merits
are very imperfectly comprehended.

V.

MR. CLEMENS has forever silenced those who affirm
that a successful author, or at any rate a man of
genius, must necessarily be a fool in business. No
reader of his books needed to be assured that he is a
man of much shrewdness, alert in observation, and

understanding what he sees. These are qualities that make the successful man of affairs, and as a man of affairs he has been even more successful than as a writer. From the publication of his "Innocents Abroad" Mr. Clemens found himself in the fortunate position of an author sure of his audience. Business He had only to write and publishers would sagacity. stand ready to bid against each other for his manuscript, and the public were equally eager for the opportunity to buy the book. Whether by good fortune or by design, the Innocents fell into the hands of a firm that sells books by subscription only. This is undoubtedly the most profitable method of publishing books for which there is a certain, a large, and an immediate sale. It did not take so shrewd a man long to discover that large as his profits were from the phenomenal sale of his books, the publisher reaped an even larger harvest of dollars. It took not much longer for Mr. Clemens to ask himself why he should not be both publisher and author, and take to himself both profits. With a man like him, to think is to plan, and to plan is to execute. And though his publishing venture has proved on the whole an unfortunate one, this result is not due to Mr. Clemens. Had he given more of his personal attention to the business, the outcome would have been different, beyond a reasonable doubt.

In private life Mr. Clemens is reputed to be one of the most genial and companionable of men. After all, the best humor, and the rarest, is good humor, and of this Mark Twain has an inexhaustible stock. His friends say that he has never done himself justice as a humorist in his books; he produces his master-pieces over a cigar with a few choice spirits. Pity it is, if this be true, that there is not a chiel amang them to take notes and prent 'em.

VIII.

FRANCIS MARION CRAWFORD.

BOSWELL tells us that when an English poet, whose very name nobody now recalls, wrote in a heroic poem —

"Who rules o'er freemen should himself be free,"

bluff old Sam Johnson mercilessly parodied the line into —

"Who drives fat oxen should himself be fat."

One hesitates to provoke a like fate by declaring that the writer of romances should himself have led a romantic life, but a certain subtle fitness of things may be acknowledged when such is the case. No writer of our day has a history of so varied adventure, so checkered experience, so sudden fame, as this American who was not born in America, and has lived fewer of his adult years in his own country than he has spent in almost any nook of Europe or Asia.

Dates are stubborn things, but when one looks over the long row of volumes written by Mr. Crawford one finds it hard to realize that he was born at Bagni di Lucca, Italy, in 1853, and is therefore barely on the shady side of forty. He is the son of Thomas

Crawford, America's most original sculptor, — who, though born in New York City, was of pure Irish

Birth and lineage. descent. His mother was a daughter of Samuel Ward, a New York banker, and a sister of Mrs. Julia Ward Howe and of genial " Uncle Sam " Ward, the favorite of Boston and Washington society. This mixture of Irish and Yankee blood, of artistic and practical temperaments, may be traced without too much fancifulness in all of Mr. Crawford's career, as well as in the lineaments of that counterfeit presentment with which his publishers have favored us. It is a frank, genial, manly face that looks out at us from this picture, suggesting an athletic frame and a capacity for the fullest enjoyment of the good things of life, while it also implies mental power and a dominant ideality. It is not the face of a mere dreamer, still less of a sensualist, but that of a well-rounded, well-balanced man, in whom mind and spirit dominate body.

After the premature death of Thomas Crawford, the widowed mother and the young lad returned to this country, and made New York their home. Young Crawford's education was begun, but he himself confesses to his friends that the school — in the neighborhood of Union Square — had for him less attractions than the circuses that were then wont to make that locality their headquarters. In course of time he picked up enough learning to enter Harvard, but did not complete his course. In the early seventies he was a student of Trinity College, Cambridge ;

later he spent two years at Karlsruhe and Heidelberg, and a final two years at the University of Rome, where he devoted himself especially to Sanskrit. While he was still not far advanced in his twenties, the financial disasters following the panic of 1873 Romantic career. wrecked the ample fortune his mother had inherited from her banker-father, and the young man was unexpectedly thrown on his own resources. It was a severe test of both character and ability, but both bore the test well. To a young man of desultory education, literary tastes, and pressing necessities, journalism offers irresistible attractions. To this profession Mr. Crawford at once turned, and after devious wanderings he became a member of the editorial staff of the " Indian Herald," of Allahabad. His knowledge of Sanskrit stood him in good stead during this Indian episode, of which he has since made excellent use in " Mr. Isaacs " and " Zoroaster." We are told that his cue, as an Indian editor, was to write down Madame Blavatsky, theosophy and kindred subjects; which is rather amusing when one remembers that his first essay in fiction was in this very realm of the marvellous and unknown that as a journalist he treated so lightly. The last ten years Mr. Crawford has spent in Italy, with occasional visits to this country, his home being a beautiful spot near Sorrento. In these facts of his history we find the key to his marked success as a novelist, as well as the sufficient explanation of his limitations.

I.

MR. CRAWFORD may be said to have stumbled upon, rather than to have chosen, his career.   After he had tired of Indian journalism, and had come to this country in search of some better occupation, he was one day spinning yarns about India to his uncle, Sam Ward.   Mr. Ward was a man of some literary ability, and of much business shrewdness; in one of these yarns he saw literary possibilities, and he advised his nephew to write it out at length and submit it to a publisher.   Such was the origin of " Mr. Isaacs," — for the nephew had, in this case, sense enough to take a bit of avuncular good advice.   The success of the book was immediate and gratifying.   It was also well deserved, for, though " Mr. Isaacs" is crude, it is a book of great promise.   There was a freshness in the subject, — Mr. Kipling had not then been heard from, — and an attractiveness about the mysterious hero, that atoned for defects obviously due to inexperience in story-writing.   It was believed by those who read the book that the author would soon obtain the technical mastery of his art; and that his native gifts, when matured and developed, would give him a high place on the roll of American novel-ists.   This hope has not been disappointed, though at times its entire fulfilment has seemed improbable.

Mr. Isaacs.

Mr. Crawford has been astonishingly prolific.   Since the appearance of his first story, in 1882, he has written and published no fewer than twenty-three other volumes, most of them of full average novel size, and has others in manuscript.   This is about a book and a half a year, a rate of production that in any case entitles him to be reckoned one of the most industrious of modern writers.   His composition is almost incredibly rapid when he once begins a story in good earnest. He must, of course, have it mapped out completely, so that nothing remains Astonishingly prolific. but the actual work of clothing his conception in words.   Then he has been known to compose a complete novel of one hundred and fifty thousand words in twenty-five consecutive working days, broken only by the intervening Sundays.   This is an average of six thousand words a day, all written with his own hand, without aid of amanuensis, stenographer, or typewriter.   Let anybody sit down some day and copy six thousand words; he will find that the mere physical labor constitutes an exhausting day's work. Let him keep this up day after day for a month, then let him add thereto in imagination the mental strain of original composition, and he will have some conception of the stupendous nature of the feat accomplished by Mr. Crawford. Most literary workers occasionally write as many as six thousand words in a day, as a sort of *tour de force*, but this is one of those things that we look back upon as matter of just pride. Who of us ever dreams of keeping this up for any number of consecutive days?

II.

IT is not enough, however, that an author be industrious; we also demand that what he does shall be worth doing, and shall be done with intelligent purpose. The late excellent Anthony Trollope to the **Genius wanted.** contrary notwithstanding, a big piece of shoemaker's-wax on the seat of one's chair is not the chief condition of success as a writer of fiction. It is important first of all that an author have something to say, something worth saying, and that he know how to say it; that granted, the wax may be very useful in getting it said, but that lacking, all the diligent labor in the world will result in quires of nothings, nothing worth. " Cudgel thy brains no more about it," says the grave-digger in " Hamlet," " for your dull ass will not mend his pace with beating." If Mr. Crawford's books do not show genius, they at least show a cleverness that cannot be expressed in units of labor. Whatever may have been the case in the beginning, his later stories show the touch of the conscious artist, and we shall do well to consider the theory on which he avowedly works.

For himself, he declines to be classified either as realist or romancer, since, in his view, a good novel should combine romance and reality in just propor- **Neither realist nor romancer.** tions, and neither element need shut out the other. Every-day life would be a very dull affair without something of romance, .and decidedly incoherent without reality; so that the novel that excludes either cannot be a true representation of life. Mr. Crawford's artistic creed is not complex: the novel must deal chiefly with love, a passion in which all men and women are interested; it must be clean and sweet, since its tale is for all mankind; it must be interesting; its realism must be of three dimensions, not flat and photographic; its romance must be truly human. What he tries to do is to "make little pocket-theatres out of words." In short, to his mind fiction is intimately allied to the <sub-note>His artistic creed.</sub-note> drama — if, indeed, these are not essentially one art, applied to different conditions of expression. To criticise this theory of fiction would lead us too far afield, and might be unprofitable in any event; what concerns our present purpose far more than its truth is the inquiry, How successful and how consistent has been the application of this theory to the actual work of novel-writing?

III.

MR. CRAWFORD'S stories may be classified as novels and romances. A "novel" may be defined as a more or less realistic fiction, a serious attempt to represent life as it is. By "romance" one understands a tale in which the illusion of probability is for the most part successfully maintained, while the story yet contains elements or incidents that on sober reflection one decides to be, if not contrary to fact, yet transcending

all ordinary experience and setting the probabilities
Crawford's   quite at defiance.   Stories whose leading
romances.   motive or turning point or chief interest
depends upon something marvellous, mysterious,
beyond ordinary human knowledge, not to say distinctly supernatural, are romances.   To illustrate by
reference to models now classic in the literature of
fiction, Hawthorne is the typical romancer, while
Thackeray is the typical novelist.   Mr. Crawford has
tried his hand at both species of fiction, not once but
many times.   In " Mr. Isaacs " he makes free use of
the marvels of Oriental theosophy, treating seriously
for the purposes of his art that which as a journalist
he had made the butt of numberless flouts and gibes
and jeers.   In " The Witch of Prague " the plot turns
on the latest theories of hypnotism and the far-reaching
possibilities of a new psychological science.   These
are the most conspicuous instances, and the most
successful by far, of an ability to construct a powerful
and interesting story out of materials which in the
hands of a less skilful writer would have produced
only an effect of *grotesquerie* or something much worse.
It is a short step from the impressive and the thrilling
to the ridiculous, and nothing is more fatal than to
produce an effect of burlesque when one would be
tragic.   Mr. Crawford somehow compels us to take
his marvels seriously while we are reading them,
however we may scout them when we lay the book
down, because he seems to take them with so tremendous seriousness himself.   There is none of that

cynical by-play of Thackeray's, in which we are now and again informed that we are only gazing on a puppet-show, not at life itself; no prestidigitateur ever kept up the illusion better, or more gravely pretended to his audience that his feats are the result, not of manual dexterity, but of mysterious powers with which he has been in some extraordinary way endowed.

These romances are clever, perhaps they exhibit Mr. Crawford's cleverness at its best; for, surely, the more intrinsically improbable a tale is, the greater the skill of the story-teller who persuades us to accept it as real, even during the telling of it. **His novels.** Still, one may confess to a juster appreciation and a higher enjoyment of the novels in which only ordinary men and women appear, whose plots violate no man's notion of the probable, but adjust themselves readily to the experience of life each reader has gained. Some one has said of this work of Mr. Crawford's that it includes the best and the worst novel ever written by an American, — meaning by the best " Saracinesca," and by the worst " An American Politician." More readers will, perhaps, subscribe to the latter half of this saying than to the former. There have been, possibly, a few worse books than this story of American political life, — one does not care to inquire too curiously about that; but if so they must be very bad. The truth is, that in-writing this story the novelist ventured out of his depth. No amount of cleverness can supply the place of knowledge, and Mr. Crawford does not know his own country and its ways. How, indeed, should he? He has never lived here, — for any length of time, that is to say, — and he knows his countrymen only in a superficial, which is always a false, way. In "The Three Fates" he made a second venture in this field, and again failed, — not quite so disastrously as before, it is true, but still failed. To be sure, the book was praised by a critic of some pretensions, as a felicitous picture of New York life. Mr. Crawford's New York friends should beseech him not to lay that flattering unction to his soul. It is not a picture of New York life, though as a travesty it may be allowed to be not without merit. But the author did not set out to write a travesty; he aimed at portraiture. He did not succeed; he never will succeed until he knows America and things American as he knows Rome and the Romans. He is still a young man, and has ample time to make the acquaintance of his countrymen. Let us hope that he will do so, and that he will then give us such studies of life in New York and Boston as he has given us of life in Rome. One is encouraged in this hope by a remark that he is credited with having lately made: "I think there is a richer field for the novelist in the United States than in Europe. There are more original characters to be found here, and they are in greater variety."

Mr. Crawford's Romans are convincing to one who knows nothing whatever about Rome, which

Two failures.

means all but a few score of Americans. No traveller, not even one who spends months in Rome, can
know enough about the city to say with _{Knows his}
authority that these books are or are not _{Rome.}
true to the life. To say that, one must know the
city like a native. He must have the *entrée* to the
most exclusive society; he must have the personal
confidence of people with whom most Americans
never get so far as to exchange a word; he must
know their family life, their pleasures, their prejudices, their very souls, in a word. For the acquiring
of this knowledge Mr. Crawford had one qualification
that is rare among American dwellers in Rome;
though of Protestant parentage, sometime during
his wanderings about the world he embraced the
Roman Catholic religion, and is a devout son of
the Church. It is not too much to say that no
Protestant will ever be admitted to the intimate association with great Roman families that is apparent
on every page of his three greatest novels.

One risks no contradiction in applying this term
to "Saracinesca," "Sant' Ilario," and "Don Orsino,"
— a trio of stories that no American novelist can be
fairly said to have surpassed. One is almost inclined,
in view of these three books, to modify a _{An unsurpassed}
little the opinion expressed concerning Mr. _{trio.}
Howells, that he is easily the first of American novelists. First, he is, on the whole, beyond doubt, but
not quite "easily;" it is no case of "Eclipse is first
and the rest are nowhere," for, by virtue of these

three books, Mr. Crawford is an uncommonly good second. And the elder novelist is first rather because of the sustained excellence of his writings than because he has risen to any higher level. Mr. Howells has written no novel that one would be willing to say is better than " Saracinesca," but Mr. Crawford has written many that are worse.

These three books are the history of a patrician family of modern Rome, and together form a single story. The history begins with the Rome of '65 and ends about the year 1888, with a possibility of further development hereafter. Mr. Crawford is evidently

The Saraci-   fond of Don Orsino, has taken immense
nescas.   pains with his portraiture, and can hardly have taken leave of him for good. The young man is little more than twenty-one; he has just escaped ruin in those great building speculations after which Rome went mad for a time ; he has just passed through his first grand passion, — he is, in fine, far too interesting a personage, and his future contains too many delightful possibilities, for his creator to abandon him. In the mean time, some of us find his family even more delightful. The old Prince Saracinesca is positively delicious, and Corona, his daughter-in-law, is charming. It is among the highest society that the reader moves in these books ; for the time being he lives in great palaces, he assists at Embassy balls and other high " functions," he becomes a spectator at a duel between a prince and a count, he is admitted to a private audience with Cardinal Anto-

nelli, he even has a glimpse of a revolution from the patrician point of view. When one comes to review the acquaintances he has made he finds among them all but two untitled men, — one a painter, the other an architect; and the latter exists only to shield the name of his patrician partner from public view. And one can think of no higher praise to bestow on Mr. Crawford than to say that in all this he escapes the faintest taint of snobbery. Every reader of fiction will recall Lord Beaconsfield's "Lothair," and perhaps will remember even better Bret Harte's clever travesty of it in his "Condensed Novels." Lord Beaconsfield also deals almost ex- _{Beaconsfield's Lothair.} clusively with dukes and earls and countesses, but in a way to suggest ignorance of the great people he described. His tawdry magnificence first amuses and finally disgusts the judicious reader. Mr. Crawford's is the antipodes of this style of writing. He chooses to write of princes, it is true, and of surroundings befitting their rank and wealth, but he describes them simply and easily, as if he had been familiar with them from his earliest years. And when he chooses he writes of other orders of Roman society with equal simplicity and fidelity.

IV.

MR. CRAWFORD avows that the ideal novel must be clean and sweet, if it is to tell its story to all mankind. This is the only manly creed, yet he avows it somewhat shamefacedly and with an apparent longing that it might be otherwise. We are, he says, men and women, and we have the thoughts of men and women, and not of school-girls; yet the school-girl practically decides what we are to hear at the theatre, and, so far as our language is concerned, determines to a great extent what we are to read. It is well for us all that Mr. Crawford has the school-girl usually in his mind's eye, if his "To Leeward" is a sample of what we may expect from our American novelists when they lose sight of the school-girl. It is very thin ice, indeed, that he skates over in this book, and the reader is relieved at the end to find that he has not broken through into a very slough of vileness. With this single exception Mr. Crawford's books may be safely commended *virginibus puerisque.*

The school-girl arbiter.

After all, is there not a good deal of humbug in that complaint of Thackeray's, echoed now and then by other novelists, that nobody nowadays dares to paint a man? — meaning, of course, a rake. The English and American tradition of decency is less of a restraint on the art of fiction than the French tradition of indecency. And the French novelist has the excuse of a sort of necessity, while the English or American writer who is indecent is guilty of gratuitous wallowing in filth. How does one justify this hard saying? It is a very simple matter, and may be done in the squeezing of a lemon. The novel, as Mr. Crawford tells us, must

Indecency of French fiction.

deal mainly with the passion of love. The inter-
course of English and American youths of both
sexes is practically unrestrained, and their marriages
are commonly preceded by a somewhat prolonged
courtship and are founded on affection. Here is the
amplest material for the art of the novelist. In
French society, on the contrary, girls are brought
up in the strictest seclusion, and marriages are ar-
ranged by parents on a purely business basis. It
may be true that these marriages turn out quite as
well as those of England or America, — the revela-
tions of our divorce courts strongly confirm those
who so assert, — but it is evident that there is no
material for romance in the French pre-matrimonial
customs. The only passion of love from which the
French novelist can extract dramatic situations and
thrilling interest is a guilty passion, and this is why
French fiction represents the breach of the A baseless
seventh commandment as more honored plaint.
than its observance. The English and American
novelists have the advantage every way, and they
speak to deaf ears when they ask our sympathy
because of the hard condition under which they
work, of showing some respect for the laws of God
and the decencies of life. Mr. Crawford's instinct is
better than his theory in regard to the dominance
of the school-girl in fiction.

The author of "Saracinesca" is one of the few
living American writers who have a European reputation equal to their standing at home. His books

have been translated into most of the languages of Europe, for the most part without his consent or profit. Being a polyglot himself, and speaking several languages as fluently as his own, he has accomplished one feat never paralleled by an American. His "Zoroaster" and "Marzio's Crucifix" he wrote in French as well as in English; and in recognition of their especial merit, and of the worth of his books in general, the French Academy a few years ago awarded him a prize of one thousand francs, — an honor as unique as it was well merited.

A polyglot writer.

Mr. Crawford has not yet reached the maturity of his powers, and we may fairly expect him to do much better work than he has yet done. His progress in art has been marked, and the past three years especially have shown a great advance over what he has done before. He produces at a rate that would be ruinous to one of less fertile mind and vigorous frame, but though his writing sometimes shows marks of haste, it is never raw and crude. He takes time to work out his conceptions thoroughly before he puts pen to paper, and where that is done comparative rates of composition are rather significant of idiosyncrasies of character than tests of relative excellence. The best work is not infrequently done at furious speed, while that over which toilful hours are spent has often not life enough in it to save it from putrefaction. Still,

His future.

Mr. Crawford's books lack the perfection of form that seldom is reached without long and loving labor. Let us hope that he may yet learn Michelangelo's secret that trifles make perfection, though perfection is no trifle. He is a man of genius, beyond question, and he has but to continue the progress he has already made to produce work that the world will never willingly let die.

IX.

FRANCES HODGSON BURNETT.

HAVE we, then, no women who are worthy of mention in the goodly company of American writers of to-day? the reader of these papers may ask. Yea, verily. *Place aux dames!* They have been kept waiting far too long. The order of these studies is not intended to be taken as a judgment of comparative merit. The practice of classifying authors and ticketing them with their relative rank

Unprofitable is doubtless amusing to those who do it, criticism. and may possibly be instructive to others — though in a very different way from that intended by the ticketers — but it is scarcely more conclusive than debate on the ancient question, "Which is preferable, summer or winter?" It is a sort of criticism that tells much more about the critic than about the authors criticised, and should be eschewed in self-protection.

I.

PROBABLY nobody will dispute Mrs. Burnett's right to a high place among American writers on the ground that she is of English birth. Though a native of

Manchester, and familiar with life in Lancashire, her parents came to this country while she was "a slip of a girl," before her character had taken form. Thus, while her early recollections have supplied her with literary material of which she has made good use, in sympathies and convictions she is genuinely American, perhaps more ardent in her patriotism than many an "heir of all the ages, in the foremost files of time,"—the proper description of a native American. Whether exacting foreign critics admit that she is truly "American" may be doubted, since she neither spells phonetically, nor deals in broad, exaggerated humor. We who have lived here all our lives, and are consequently so blinded by proximity to things American that we do not really see them as they are, may be pardoned for insisting that Mrs. Burnett is one of us.

English born,

American bred.

That Miss Hodgson should become an author seems to have been ordained from the beginning. In that charming autobiography of hers which so delightfully entertained the readers of "Scribner's Magazine," under the title of "The One I Knew Best of All,"—she tells us that from her earliest recollection she lived in an ideal world, and was an unconscious playwright and romancer even in the nursery. She could not see anybody who impressed her at all without making him or her a character in these dramas and romances, and inventing all sorts of deliciously

"Lisped in numbers."

impossible adventures for them. To set these on
paper was no great exploit when she became a little
older, and she scribbled tales and verses for her
own amusement, with no thought of doing anything
remarkable. Her mother was sensible enough,
even when impressed by the talent of the child's
performance, to suppress signs of gratification, so
that the budding author escaped the conceit with
which the ordinary infant phenomenon is eaten up.
While she was still in her "teens" Miss Hodgson
began to write stories for publication, moved thereto
by desire for fame perhaps, but still more, one conjectures, by the prosaic desire to put money in her
purse. In 1867 there were few periodicals to which
a young writer could send stories with any prospect
of payment, and when payment was received it was
a sum that in these days would be considered ridi-
culously small. It happened that "Peterson's
Magazine" was the first to accept and print one of
Miss Hodgson's stories, and thereafter she was for
several years a quite regular contributor to that
periodical.

II.

ONE of the chief objects that the founders of
"Scribner's Monthly" proposed to themselves was
the encouragement of American literature, and among the most notable of their
discoveries must be placed Mrs. Burnett. In 1872
her first story appeared in the magazine, — "Surly

Tim's Troubles,"—and it proved that the young author had become master of her powers, and was ready to do better work than the simple stories she had hitherto produced. A somewhat prolonged silence followed this publication, however, for another love had come to divide Frances Hodgson's affection for literature. In 1873 she was married to Luan M. Burnett, M.D., then a rising physician of Knoxville, Tenn. Since 1875 their home has been in Washington, where Dr. Burnett has won an enviable reputation and practice as a specialist in diseases of the eye. He is in no danger, therefore, of being known to the world only as "the husband of Mrs. Burnett, the famous novelist, you know," which of all fates must be the most detestable to a man of any spirit or brains.

Mrs. Burnett's pen was not idle while she was making trial of her new vocation of wife and mother; for in 1877 appeared "That Lass o' Lowrie's," having first had an honorable career as a serial in "Scribner's Monthly." This gave the author her first real taste of fame, and the book was so great a success that more substantial reward was hers at once. From that time on the world has gone well with her, if a large bank account and the praise of men can make a woman happy. As each of her books has appeared, it has been greeted with a chorus of approbation, and even when the critics have doubted, as critics sometimes will, the public has stood by its favorite and bought

without a qualm of doubt. The later novels from
her pen have been: "Haworth's" (1879),
"Louisiana" (1880), "A Fair Barbarian"
(1881), and "Through One Administration" (1883).
Popular as all these have been, none of them has
quite equalled "That Lass o' Lowrie's" in the
favor of the reading public. This has run through
edition after edition, and still has a sale little
diminished by the lapse of time. It well deserves
this perennial favor. There is about the story a
freshness, a keenness of observation, an accuracy of
character-drawing almost photographic, and a charm
of style that have been equalled in few American
novels, and perhaps surpassed in none. The scene
is in that •Lancashire which was familiar to the
author in her childhood, and therefore this is
in a sense the least American of all her stories. In
spite of this, the book took fast hold of American
readers, and their first verdict is not likely ever to
be reversed.

Without being a partisan of any school of art,
Mrs. Burnett was in this story a realist of the
straitest sect, — unconsciously so in part,
no doubt, for one cannot credit her with
having a theory to serve. She set out to tell a
story true to the life she had herself observed, and
she peopled her book with such men and women as
she had actually known. She tells us, in the autobiography to which reference has already been
made, how the heroine was suggested to her, — the

face of a girl whom she once met and of whom she knew nothing, haunting her for years, and irre-sistibly suggesting a train of adventures that must at some time get themselves written down. But while fancy thus supplied the warp of the tale, actual minute observation formed its woof. The people of this book are real people; they have been studied from life by one who has a wonderful faculty of close observation, an indelible memory, and an exceptional power of conveying to her readers what she has seen.

Mrs. Burnett also showed in this book — she had given us glimpses of the fact before — that she is one of the chosen few who have the _{Her gift of} innate faculty of expression. It is as ^{style.} impossible to say in what consists the gift of style as to define the perfume of the rose or the har-monies of Beethoven. It is incommunicable, it defies analysis, it can only be felt and enjoyed. It is not essential to the making of a successful or even a great novelist, — witness Dickens, Reade, and Collins, men of great gifts as writers of fiction, differing wonderfully in method and effect, but alike in that none of them was ever able to write a page that one would read a second time for its charm, while they became insufferable whenever they tried to do a bit of really fine writing. But whatever Mrs. Burnett writes is worth reading, quite apart from its matter, for the manner in which she says things. Her books would be enjoy-

able in a way, if they violated every canon of the art
of fiction.   Though she were to write nonsense we
should still read, merely to see how delightfully it
is possible for a writer to say foolish nothings.   But
she does not write nonsense, — quite the contrary.
The praise she has received has not disturbed her
mental equilibrium, and has never betrayed her
into a display of illusory omniscience.   Womanly
as ever, painstaking in her art, not concealing her
natural pleasure at her success, but not unduly
elated by it, she has gone on with her work, each
year enlarging her fame and gaining fresh laurels.
For if the critic agree with the verdict of the
public, that on the whole she has never surpassed
and perhaps never equalled her first great success,
each subsequent volume has shown her mastery of
the art of fiction, and has displayed it in a different
field, adding to the first triumph a series of lesser
conquests, and demonstrating the breadth of her
knowledge, her sympathy, her humanity.

III.

A GREATER triumph than she had won in her
books for grown-up people was in store for Mrs.
Burnett when she began to write for the little folks.
Little Lord   The exploits and sayings of one of her
Fauntleroy.   own boys suggested to her the story of
"Little Lord Fauntleroy" (1886), which was, with-
out question, the most successful book for children

ever written by an American. It extended the author's fame more than another sort of book could have spread it, for in capturing the hearts of the little ones she won those of fathers and mothers the whole country over; and thousands who would never have heard of the author of "That Lass o' Lowrie's" feel themselves on terms of familiar acquaintance with the author of "Little Lord Fauntleroy."

On the whole, the book must be pronounced more successful as an article of commerce than as a work of art. It has but one defect, to be sure, but that is most serious, abso- ^{Faultily fault-less.} lutely fatal in fact, — the hero of the tale is too faultily faultless. There surely never was a live boy, since boys first were, so absolutely perfect as Fauntleroy. The best boy in the world sometimes tears his clothes, musses his hair, has fits of ill-temper, and fails of perfect obedience and unselfishness. But Fauntleroy is without any of these failings; he is always irreproachably dressed, exquisitely polite, and his conduct is without a flaw. He reminds one of that nursery heroine, the little girl who —

> "When she was good she was very, very good,
> And when she was bad she was horrid;"

only, he reminds us solely of the first half of her character, for he is never bad by any chance or mischance. He is so very, very good, indeed, that he is not quite human. We must take him, not for a picture of a real boy, but for the author's ideal of what a boy ought to be. Masculine critics may, perhaps, be pardoned for saying that the ideal lacks something. Fauntleroy is far too much of a mamma's darling; he just comes short of being a prig,— comes short by so narrow a space that it may be questioned if he does not sometimes overstep the line. In spite of her faculty of observation, her sympathetic quality as an artist, and her experience of motherhood, Mrs. Burnett has not quite plucked the heart out of the mystery of boy nature, and a little dash of masculine roughness, a *soupçon* of naughtiness, would have made Fauntleroy more human. And though this might have lessened his attractiveness to fond mammas, the not less fond papas would have had less difficulty in recognizing the picture.

It is not to be considered remarkable that, from the appearance of the first instalment of this story in "St. Nicholas" to its publication in book form, the interest of readers should have been continuous and even increasing. The story is told with the perfection of art; the author's charm of style was never more apparent than in this book. The children, who were her chief readers at first, might not have been fully conscious of this charm, though they doubtless felt its power, but their elders were more intelligently, yet hardly more heartily, appreciative. Since then Mrs. Burnett

Adored by the children.

has been sure of her audience among either old or young in America whenever she cared to break silence. Several books for children have succeeded the story of Fauntleroy, such as "Sarah Crewe," "Little Saint Elizabeth" and other stories, and "Giovanni and the Other." Had these books not been obliged to undergo comparison with her first extraordinary success, they might have been pronounced excellent; under the circumstances they have probably been something of a disappointment to her public. The public always expects that an author, having once struck twelve, should go on striking twelve indefinitely, and even lazily wonders why he does not strike thirteen. The demand is unreasonable, but since it exists authors must submit to be judged by readers who have this prepossession. One must either go on record, like "Single-speech Hamilton," as the writer of one brilliantly successful book, or be content to have all subsequent writings declared to be inferior to that by which he first gained reputation. It will be a generation or two hence before just notions are entertained, not merely regarding the relative rank of living authors, but the relative value and significance of each writer's books. This at least is to be said now for Mrs. Burnett's later children's books: they are, from the artist's point of view, superior to the more popular Fauntleroy, because truer to life. She understands girls, and her girls are much more human than her impossible boy hero. This is

Other books for young readers.

not the popular verdict, but one is persuaded that it will be the ultimate judgment alike of readers and of critics.

IV.

COMPARATIVELY few of our American writers of fiction, as has already been noted, have won success on the stage. How far Mrs. Burnett has had the assistance of more experienced playwrights, one cannot say, but such collaboration could in no case have extended beyond those technicalities that are pitfalls for the unwary. Her plays have been adaptations of her most successful stories, and their stage success has equalled, perhaps surpassed, their vogue in print. This has been due in the main to their intrinsic merits, but in one case an extraordinary "run" was due to the fortunate production of the play. One refers, of course, to the dramatization of Fauntleroy's story. By good chance the manager who produced the play lighted upon a very bright and charming little girl, of phenomenal dramatic gifts, to take the leading part in the play. She dressed and acted the part of Fauntleroy to perfection, and succeeded in divesting the character of that unreal air which mars the perfection of the story. The living Fauntleroy seemed more human, less priggish; the art of the little actress was convincing, where the art of the novelist had failed to convince.

No doubt this dramatic success has been gratify-

A dramatic success.

ing to the author, because it brought her a wider and well-deserved fame, and still more because it has made her, comparatively speaking, a rich woman. The rewards of author- Its reward. ship are not excessive, even in the case of the most fortunate; lawyers or physicians of medium abilities may be named by the score, in any one of our great cities, whose yearly income far surpasses that of the best paid man of letters in the United States. When any one of the profession, therefore, gets something like his due reward, it is cause for general rejoicing in the craft, not for jealousy and gnashing of teeth. Every such success brings nearer the day when the profession of letters will be as well paid, for work of the same grade, as the pro-fessions of medicine or the law; when the salary of a millionnaire's cook will not exceed the copyright value of a work that from the day of its publication takes its place among American classics.

Mrs. Burnett's dramatic success had one result for which all who favor pure and innocent amuse-ments may well be grateful. Many people One sequel. who had never entered a theatre in their lives went to see Fauntleroy, overcome by the per-suasion of their children, and "snatched a fearful joy" in the playhouse, half-persuaded still that they were committing a deadly sin. They were shown by the most effective of object lessons that the stage is not necessarily the corrupt and corrupting thing they had been taught to believe it to be, —

that it may be made, not merely innocent and amusing, but elevating and ennobling. If good people appiied to books the logic they apply to the stage, if they refused to read any books because so many bad books are printed, there would soon be no readers but the vicious and the vile, and so in a little while only bad books would be made. Mrs. Burnett's little play was a missionary force that did wonders in the breaking down of almost invincible prejudice founded on ignorance and misinformation.

It is a curious fact that though she lived for ten years, ten years of the most impressionable part of her life in Tennessee, the work of Mrs. Burnett bears almost no trace of this experience. One would think that she must know the Tennessee folk as well as Miss Murfree, but her books are concerned almost wholly with the Lancashire of her childhood, or the American cities in which her maturer years have been spent. One can hardly account for her ignoring of this rich material, for she was in the field and had made a name for herself before Miss Murfree, and there was no question of another's priority to hold her in check. It may be, for Mrs. Burnett should have many years of literary work before her, that in some future romance this mine may be worked by her, and that we shall be made richer by acquaintance with some Joan of Tennessee. At any rate, we are warranted in expecting from her greater things than she has yet done.

Her ignoring of Tennessee.

X.

CHARLES EGBERT CRADDOCK.

VETERAN readers of the "Atlantic," when they cut the leaves of the number for May, 1878, had a fresh sensation. In the "Contents" on the familiar yellow cover they read, "The Dancin' Party at Harrison's Cove, by Charles Egbert Craddock." The title and the name suggested little, — the name was absolutely new to *The first story.* every reader, — but those who read the story found that the writer had opened an entirely fresh vein in American literature. Harrison's Cove, it turned out, was a settlement among the mountains of Tennessee, now first made known to the world at large; and the story was concerned with the fortunes of a type of mankind quite new to literature.

From time to time other stories appeared from the same writer. Their merit was recognized, and the name of Craddock was enrolled on the list of our rising authors. Finally, in 1884, eight of these tales were gathered into a volume *In the Tennessee Mountains.* inscribed with the title, "In the Tennessee Mountains." On a copy of this book, printed in 1892, one finds the legend, dear to the heart of authors, "Twenty-second edition." To be sure, "edition" means little or much in the American trade, but in this case it is understood to mean one thousand copies. The author whose first book sells at this rate evidently has the game in his hands.

So far, singularly little was known of the writer of these tales. The fact became public after a while that Charles Egbert Craddock was a pseudonym, and that the writer's real name was M. N. Murfree, but this was just enough light to make the darkness visible. Neither editor nor publisher had any acquaintance with him save by letter. No other American author knew anything about him. His post-office address was St. Louis; and it was evident that he must at some time have lived among the folk and the scenes that he described so graphically; but beyond this nobody had any information. Handwriting, according to Poe and others, is an infallible index of character. Mr. Craddock's chirography would have indicated to any interpreter a bold, masculine, adventurous nature, — it was so free, so decided, so heavy. Indeed, the expenditure of ink is so lavish as to suggest that the writer used the sharp end of a stick, *à la* John Chinaman, instead of a pen, for no goose ever hatched, one would think, could furnish a quill capable of such execution. Mr. Aldrich, then editor of the "Atlantic," used to crack his jokes on this peculiarity. "I wonder," he remarked one day, "if Craddock has laid in his

The mysterious author.

winter's ink; perhaps we could get a serial from him."

What was the sensation one spring day in 1885 when there walked into the editorial office of the "Atlantic" a demure young woman who The mystery announced herself as Charles Egbert Crad- disclosed. dock! The proverbial feather would have knocked down everybody, from editor-in-chief to office cat. A Southern girl in her twenties had fooled the 'cuteness of all Yankeedom, and brought to naught the critics with their boasted insight, and their wonderful gift of determining all sorts of obscure matters by internal evidence. Beginning with Mr. Aldrich, or even with Mr. Howells before him, and going on down to the smallest newspaper scribbler, they were all her victims. Not one of them had divined that Charles Egbert Craddock was other than he seemed.

This was a more notable achievement than appears on the face of the facts. One of the best kept literary secrets of the century was the authorship of "Scenes of Clerical Life" and "Adam Surpasses Bede." Special pains were taken to keep George Eliot. the public in the dark. For some time even Mr. John Blackwood, the editor who accepted the tales for his magazine, and the publisher who afterwards issued them in book form, was as much mystified as anybody. He was so completely taken in by the pseudonym that he addressed letters to the author, under care of Lewes, as "My dear George." To

be sure, Mr. Aldrich with his " My dear Craddock,"
quite duplicated this performance; but from the
very first there were those who divined the secret
of George Eliot, though, of course, they could not
accurately fix the personality. When the first story
appeared, Dickens suspected the author to be a
woman, while Thackeray and Mrs. Oliphant were
certain that such was the case. But no happy
instinct led anybody to guess the secret of Charles
Egbert Craddock. The name was not even suspected of being a pseudonym until this was confessed, and when so much was admitted, nobody
suspected that anything remained to be cleared up.
The author had no need of lying, as the author of
" Waverley " had, to silence prying questioners, —
there were none, since Mr. Craddock-Murfree was
accepted everywhere at his own valuation. A further element of triumph consisted in the fact that
George Eliot's hand was forced by a rival claimant
to the authorship of her books, else the attempt to
keep the secret might have continued; but the author
of the Craddock tales made her incognito good until
she no longer cared to conceal her identity, and
she chose her own time and place for a dramatic
dénouement.

I.

THE story was, of course, too good to keep, and
the identity of the already popular author was made
known to the world. From that time, though the

pseudonym still appears on title pages and in cata-
logues, the author has been best known under her
own proper cognomen. With the transpiring of the
secret a few biographical details were also made
public, though they are rather scanty.

Mary Noailles Murfree comes of the best American stock. Her great-grandfather, Hardy Murfree,
was a native of North Carolina, and a   Her lineage.
gallant soldier in the War of the Revolution. He was a subordinate of Mad Anthony
Wayne at the storming of Stony Point, — the most
brilliant action of the whole war, on either side, —
and bore himself honorably in many another contest, rising to the rank of colonel before peace was
declared. In 1807 he emigrated to the new State
of Tennessee, and settled near the present town of
Murfreesboro, which was named in his honor. Miss
Murfree was born at the family estate, Grantlands,
near Murfreesboro. It is said that while quite
young she suffered the misfortune of a stroke of
paralysis, which rendered her lame for life. She
was thus debarred from the active life and open-air
sports of other children, and turned for consolation
to books, becoming an eager student and omni-
vorous reader. The Civil War reduced the family
fortunes, and shortly after its close her father removed to St. Louis, where he engaged in the
practice of law.

This is about all that is known to the public of
this author's life; for the rest we are dependent

chiefly on conjecture and the internal evidence
afforded by her books.   It is, perhaps, a fair inference that a desire for the emoluments of literature,
rather than for its fame, influenced Miss Murfree
in her first efforts.   Dr. Johnson once said something to the effect that nobody but a fool ever wrote
anything except for pay, but this is not one of the
wisest sayings of old Ursa Major.   Doubtless the
need of bread and butter has, in modern times at
least, produced more literature than ambition, but
if that were the only motive it would be a bread-
A conscien-   and-butter literature that would be pro-
tious worker.   duced.   Though Johnson's saying was
obviously a hasty generalization founded on imperfect induction, and is not to be taken *au pied de
lettre*, it contains more than a modicum of truth.
What Miss Murfree's books warrant us in concluding is that, from whatever motive she began her
writing, she has continued because she loves her
calling, and takes honest pride in doing her work
well, irrespective of the reward.   Conscientious
workmanship can never be mistaken, and its significance is great.   No merely mercenary writer can
be an artist in words.   There is no reason why he
should be.   The annals of modern literature are full
of instances of sudden reputation won, and great
gains made by men and women who were no more
novelists than a negro kalsominer is a painter.   If
one writes to make money only or chiefly, the thing
to do is to set up a literary mill and grind out books

by the bushel, like — but every instructed reader can name half a dozen such without hesitation.

Miss Murfree's workmanship is admirable, in the first instance, because she writes from adequate knowledge of her subject. She knows the Tennessee mountains and the Tennessee people thoroughly. She has not merely mastered their surface peculiarities, such as their dialect, their dress, their mode of life, but she has seen to the bottom of their souls, and knows their inner life as well as the outer. She has not only seen, she has analyzed, combined, classified, interpreted her facts until she fully comprehends them in all their relations. If she had been a devotee of realism she might have ended with seeing and describing; as it is, while truly realistic, with a sharpness of detail almost photographic, in her fidelity to fact she does not forget the higher truth of being, and so she both understands her people and makes us understand them likewise.

But this knowledge is not enough for a novelist, or, rather, it is not possible without the previous acquisition of other knowledge, or, still again, if its acquirement is possible, it cannot be successfully communicated to others; its real nature cannot even be grasped fully by one otherwise untutored. There are scores in the Tennessee mountains who know all that Miss Murfree could see there, know it more completely, perhaps, and have made it much more a part of themselves, but

12

they could never tell it to the world; in a sense, and a very real sense, they may be said not actually to know it, for they do not know it in relation to other knowledges. Miss Murfree brought with her to the mountains and the mountain folk, the power of seeing more than an ordinary observer could find in either. She brought a cultivated mind, made impressible by natural and spiritual beauty through the study of nature, of literature, of life. Those long early years of reading and meditation had not been in vain. None see so deeply into the heart of things as those who have been in a measure secluded from the world, and have had as the instructors of their working hours and their companions in idleness the choicest minds of all ages.

II.

Miss Murfree began her work, we have already seen, as a writer of short stories, but her continu-
Short stories.   ance in this province was brief. Since the publication of "In the Tennessee Mountains," if one remembers correctly, she has never tried this kind of writing again. Probably we owe her early tales to the same cause that impelled the disguise of a pseudonym, — a lack of confidence in her powers, and a wish to make experiment in a modest way before attempting an ambitious enterprise. Her instinct must have told her very soon, however, that she had nothing to

fear, and also must have assured her that she was wasting her material in the composition of these tales. Several of them, though they seem at first reading to reach the height of excellence just as they are, on analysis disclose the fact that they are not so much complete tales as abbreviated novels. This is especially true of "Drifting Down Lost Creek," into which enough of plot and character is crowded to furnish forth a novel of full length. The skeleton is there complete, and only needs to be clothed with flesh, that is to say, with dialogue and description, to make a book equal in interest and power to any of the author's later writing. In the perfect short story the length of the tale is exactly proportioned to its content, and to expand it to the dimensions of a novel would make of it an intolerable wishy-washy dilution. Though we find a defect in some of these stories, it must be admitted that it is a fault that leans to virtue's side. Not much literary work, in these days, can be called imperfect because of its excess of riches.

It did seem, however, on her first trial of a longer flight, that a good writer of tales had been spoiled to make a poor novelist. Not that there were no good points in "Where the Battle Very like a failure. was Fought" (Boston, 1884); Miss Murfree could not, if she tried, write a book without solid merits. The book simply was not so good as we had a right to expect. Her tales had been as vigorous, as sinewy, as wholesome as her mountaineers. This was a novel of the conventional sort, with a plot of the well-worn type, and lacked the characteristic Craddock flavor. A wish to show that she could write about something else than the mountain people may have caused the author to make this mis step. Doubtless she can write about many other things, but doubtless she can write of nothing about which her public would so willingly hear. The scenes and types of her stories brought the piquant and titillating flavor of absolute novelty to the jaded palate of the novel reader; and though the taste is now familiar, it has lost none of its savor. Still less was there danger ten years ago that the public would quickly tire of the mountains and their quaint men and women.

Miss Murfree is not one of those who cannot learn in the school of experience, and she has never repeated that mistake. From that time on, in regular succession her books have come from the press showing a steady growth in artistic power.

Her books. First came "Down the Ravine" (1885), followed in the same year by "The Prophet of the Great Smoky Mountains," and at slightly longer intervals by "In the Clouds" (1886), "The Story of Keedon Bluffs" (1887), "The Despot of Brownsedge Cove" (1888), and "In the 'Stranger People's Country" (New York, 1891). This is pretty rapid production, but not too rapid for good workmanship, as the books themselves prove, and as is proved by the example of numerous other novelists, American and foreign. Slow composition does not necessarily produce work of a high quality; comparative rates of production are a test of temperament and industry rather than of excellence. There is no "scamped" work in Miss Murfree's books. She produces rapidly but not hurriedly, and no signs of slipshod or careless performance are traceable in any of her writing. So long as she keeps up to the mark she has set for herself, and thus far reached without one failure — for "Where the Battle was Fought," so far as it may be called a failure, failed because of an unwise choice of theme, not by lack of faithful labor — the more books she gives her readers the more she will gratify the most critical among them.

III.

FOUR things go to the making of a good novel: plot, dialogue, description, style. There may be other things, but these are the chief, and novelists differ from each other mainly in the relative importance they assign to these four elements and their relative skill in the use of them. Few writers are really great in more than two of these four things, and are fortunate not to fall below mediocrity in one or more of them.

Miss Murfree is not remarkable for the strength or interest of her plots; the best we can say of them is that they answer her purposes, and do not

impress the reader as unpleasantly weak. She is to be praised in that, not having a genius for in-
Plot. vention, she has risen above the temptation to strain after effects she could not gain. It is a rare grace in a writer to be content to remain simply natural, and that grace she has.

In the matter of dialogue, also, the critic must give Miss Murfree a curiously qualified commenda-
Dialogue. tion: she both reaches and falls short of the highest excellence. Here, too, she is found to be natural, which in a sense is the highest praise that could be spoken of any writer. But her characters are uncultivated people; they come of a race distinguished for rugged strength rather than for grace; to endow them with wit and humor, — save of the primitive kind, — with reflectiveness, with philosophic insight, would have been to make them caricatures of the rugged and uncouth mountaineer. By the nature of her subject-matter the author precluded herself from brilliancy of dialogue. Keen dialect, the fine play of fancy, lambent humor, scintillating wit, quotation and allusion, — all the mental charms we associate with high culture, — are out of the question in her books. For these we must go to Howells, or James, or Crawford. It is a necessity of the situation, and by the deliberate restraint Miss Murfree has put upon herself in this matter she shows an art far higher than she would have shown by yielding to the temptation to display her abilities.

It is in description alone that the author has been free to give full scope to her literary skill. In the first story of the "Atlantic" series there was a taste of her quality, in this Description. picture of an August sky: "An early moon was riding, clear and full, over this wild spur of the Alleghanies; the stars were few and very faint; even the great Scorpio lurked, vaguely outlined, above the wooded ranges; and the white mist, that filled the long, deep, narrow valley between the parallel lines of mountains, shimmered with opalescent gleams." Miss Murfree has gone on cultivating her gift, until in her last books it comes very near absolute perfection. She accomplishes some feats that are almost incredible. Who would have believed it possible, for instance, that the fleeting effects of light and shade caused by the passage of a cloud could be expressed in anything save the colors of a painter's palette, if he had not read this: "His eyes were on the stretch of barley, bending and swaying as the wind swept through its pliant blades, and shoaling from an argentine glister to green, and from green again to elusive silver glintings — what time the cove below was dark and purple and blurred, as a great white cloud hung, dazzling and opaque, high, high in the sky, and, as it passed, the valley grew gradually into distinctness again, with the privilege of the sunshine and the freedom of the wind, and all its land-marks asserted anew." Here is a scene equally fine: "He turned and looked at the gorge, as if he expected to see there the pearly disk among the dark obscurements of the night-shadowed mountains. It was instead a vista of many gleaming lights; the sunshine on the river, and the differing lustre of the water in the shadow; the fine crystalline green of the cataract, and the dazzling white of the foam and the spray; the luminous azure of the far-away peaks, and the enamelled glister of the blue sky, — all showing between the gloomy, sombre ranges close at hand."

Pages of such bits might be extracted from these later books. And yet it should not be inferred that the author has fallen a victim to her acquired facility, and bores her reader with passages inserted for mere display. Few writers show a better appreciation of the shrewd saying of the sententious Hobbes: "For words are wise men's counters, — they do but reckon by them; but they No purple patches. are the money of fools." In every case, these bits of landscape are fitted into the story so deftly as to be an inseparable part of it; they accompany and explain the acts and moods of the characters so as to justify their place in the text, and are no purple patches clumsily stitched on as an afterthought. Surely, such writing as the above bits fairly represent is entitled to the much-abused and sadly vulgarized phrase "word-painting."

It is no violent transition, certainly, to a general

consideration of Miss Murfree's style.   Simplicity,
correctness, and grace are its character-   Style.
istics.   It is true that these adjectives
apply only when the author has not her dialect fit
on; mountainese and pure English are necessarily
incompatible.   But it must be said, in justice to
her, that her dialect is quite as clever as her
ordinary English style; it is not exaggerated or
overdone, and the conventional orthography is not
unnecessarily mangled.   There are strange muta-
tions in writing as well as in dress, and literary
fashions change with quite as much bewildering
rapidity and quite as little reasonableness as the
fashions in millinery.   The rationale of fashion is
a deep subject, — if one may predicate rationality
of anything whose origin seems to be in utter
mental vacuousness, — and we are concerned at
present only with its phenomena.   An unreason-
ing vogue of dialect a few years ago has been succeeded by a prejudice against dialect, that would
be quite as unreasonable had not the reading public
been surfeited by the deluge of dialect stories produced by its first eager patronage.   But there is
dialect and dialect.   Miss Murfree's is of the best;
and, in any case, it is hard to see how she could
have written of her mountaineers on any other
terms.   Certainly, if she was to represent them as
they are, she must set them before us with their
peculiar speech.   The only question that can fairly
be raised in this case is whether it was worth while

for Miss Murfree to write stories about the Tennessee
mountains at all.   As to that, but one verdict can
be expected of her readers.   If there are any who
think otherwise, the world of letters is all before
them where to choose.

We could ill spare Miss Murfree's contribution
to fiction.   It is racy of the soil.   The most exacting among our British censors will not venture to
deny to her books the right to the distinctive
epithet, American.

XI.

ELIZABETH STUART PHELPS.

LORD BYRON once said, in describing the sudden fame that came to him from the publication of the first part of " Childe Harold's Pilgrimage," ".I awoke next morning and found myself famous." There was almost as much truth as hyperbole in the saying, and the same remark might have been made by the author of " The Gates Ajar." When that book first appeared, more than twenty-five years ago, it attained a popularity of the most extensive and impressive sort. There were some weeks, according to the story told of it by its publisher, when the fate of the book seemed trembling in the balance; then all at once the sales showed

Sudden fame.

a phenomenal increase, and advanced by leaps and bounds. Twenty editions were sold within a single year. The book was on every table, and its discussion was on every lip. The furore it caused was even greater than that provoked recently by the publication of " Robert Elsmere." The theology underlying the book was ardently defended by some and fiercely criticised by others. Long articles were written against it in the religious newspapers, and ministers made it the theme of sermons, mostly minatory and anathema-breathing, and dreadful things were said of the author's heterodoxy.   It was, in short, one of the notable literary successes of our time; and whatever one may think of the book, now that a quarter-century has passed away, and the time for a cool judgment has come, it still remains a literary success of the first magnitude.

I.

Now, notwithstanding Dogberry's *obiter dictum* that "reading and writing come by nature," nothing is more certain than the fact that a book of this kind does not get itself written by accident.   Elizabeth Stuart Phelps, when she wrote "The Gates Ajar," had served an apprenticeship of some length in litera-ture.   She began to write for the press at
A born author.
thirteen years of age, and was already the author of a dozen volumes, stories for children mostly, of the usual Sunday-school type — no, of an unusual type.   She was the daughter of Austin Phelps, the instructor of Andover theologues for forty years in sacred rhetoric, and the writer of a small library of books whose brilliant and pungent style has been admired by two generations of readers.   Her mother was Elizabeth Stuart, — daughter of Moses Stuart, another name inseparably connected with the history of Andover, — herself the author of many books, mostly fiction with a religious motive.   Miss Phelps

thus breathed the atmosphere of letters from her infancy, and alike by inherited instinct and by careful
training was fitted for a literary career. That she
should begin one was to be expected; that she should
be successful it was perhaps equally safe to prophesy;
what nobody could have foreseen, herself least of all
probably, was that when she had barely arrived at the
dignity of young-ladyhood she should become one of
the most famous of American authors. This was in
part, to be sure, the result of good fortune, but it was
also the reward of earnest endeavor and conscientious
literary workmanship.

It is something of a puzzle to one who now reads
" The Gates Ajar " for the first time, and even to one
who re-reads it after many years, to understand the
secret of its immediate and wide and enduring popularity. It is not a novel, and it is not a The Gates
religious treatise, but something half-way Ajar.
between the two. It might be described as a sort of
prose " In Memoriam " with a thread of story. In the
form of a diary it gives the meditations and experiences of a young woman who has lately lost a
brother to whom she was tenderly attached. The
divine purposes in the affliction of men, the discipline
of sorrow, the grounds of faith in immortality, the
nature of the future life, especially the latter, are the
themes to which attention is chiefly directed. These
are not subjects that might be expected to rouse
general interest. The *a priori* reasoner would have
been likely to forecast disaster, or at best a very

moderate success, for any book that discussed questions of this nature; and in the present day he might
be right. The conditions were different, however,
twenty-five years ago. As is the case with all greatly
successful books, "The Gates Ajar" struck a chord
in the people's hearts that only needed the touch of a
Its appeal to   master's hand to respond. It appeared soon
the heart.   after the Civil War, when in almost every
household there was still mourning for some loved
and lost one. Tens of thousands of sore hearts were
asking themselves just the questions that the supposi-
titious writer of this book kept asking. If Miss Phelps
did not give a final reply to these questionings, she
helped many to a stronger faith in the reality and
blessedness of the future life, and a hope of reunion
with the lost, — a reunion that should be conscious,
intelligent, and blissful, as well as unending. She
essayed, and with much success, —

> " To pluck the amaranthine flower
> Of faith, and round the sufferer's temples bind
> Wreaths that endure affliction's heaviest shower,
> And do not shrink from sorrow's keenest wind."

No wonder, therefore, the book found readers; the
seed fell into good soil, already prepared for it, and
that it should germinate and fructify was in the ordinary course of nature.

But the book owed its great vogue to another cause,
that no longer exists. In the sixties what passed for
orthodox theology was practically silent about the

future life.   Beyond maintaining with great energy
the immortality of the soul and the eternal Glimpses of the
punishment of the wicked, it practically silent world.
ignored all the questions that cluster about the word
"eschatology." Not only was theology silent on these
themes, but the pulpit was likewise dumb.   Yet the
people were anxiously questioning and doubting, and
from the source to which they might naturally have
turned for light they met with chilling silence or stern
rebuke.   "The Gates Ajar" boldly attacked problems
that the pulpits and theological chairs feared or
ignored, and while it did not say the last word on
any of them, it did in many cases say what was to
most people the first word of comfort they had ever
heard.

These papers are not theological disquisitions, and
it is not necessary, therefore, to discuss the grave
question whether this book is, as has been so often
charged, "tainted with Swedenborgianism." Its "Sweden-
What is taken for Swedenborgianism in borgianisms."
the book of Miss Phelps, by those who interpret everything with absolute literalism, is probably nothing
more than a speaking in parables on her part.   When
she says, for instance, that the saints will have pianos
in heaven, only the literal-minded will mistake her
meaning, — such people as cannot appreciate humor
and need to have all their poetry translated into bald
prose before it is level to their intellects.   In the
Revelation we read of harps in heaven, and if the harp
of the first century, why not the pianoforte of the

nineteenth? Things like this mystified some readers
and disquieted others, but it is not likely that many
were stumbled by them. At all events, whatever
incidental harm might have been done by trifles of
this sort was largely overbalanced by the great and
positive good accomplished through the book.

II.

MISS PHELPS deserved her suddenly gained fame,
but if it had rested on no other basis than this one
book it would have proved evanescent. "The Gates
Ajar" is even now, one fears, mainly of historic interest. Though it still is a good selling book, it is not
so completely in touch with the spiritual needs of the
Not a single   time as when it was first printed, and by
success.   the time a third generation of readers has
come on the stage it promises to be outgrown. This
is the fate of books that address themselves to religious emotion and one phase of religious thought.
It was an open question in her case whether she would
be content with this fame, or would strive after higher
things. A first great triumph like this may have
either of two effects on the writer, especially on a
young and impressionable writer : it may be a stimulus,
or a paralysis. In far too many cases one great stroke
of fortune either puffs a writer up with conceit or ter-
rifies him by its very greatness, so that he is never fit
for a higher flight. The writer who has in him the

true stuff, while grateful for the praise and appreciation that he has won, is spurred on to greater industry
and more concentrated effort. It was so with Miss
Phelps. She was neither spoiled nor frightened, but
girded herself for other and better work. For fifteen
years she abandoned the theme through which she
first gained the ear of the public, and devoted herself
to fiction, averaging a book a year during this time.
The culmination of this series of books was " The
Story of Avis," which, in the minds of most readers,
will long continue to be the favorite, though one or
two others may press it rather closely.

Miss Phelps is equally successful as a writer of
short stories and in longer tales. She has become a
thorough literary workman, and she never slights her
work. Her plots are fairly good, though never com-
plicated, and she peoples her books with persons
whom it is good to know. Her knowledge of human
nature is respectably wide and deep ; and though it
does not impress one as exhaustive, it is satisfactory
as far as it goes. From her books one gets Her short tales.
the impression that she has lived a rather
shut-in life, circumscribed by conditions of health and
of family duty that have made it difficult to see more
than a small part of the world. But Miss Phelps certainly knows her New England well; she knows the
dialect, the customs, the ways of thinking, the spiritual
needs of the Yankee, especially the Yankee girl and
woman, with a comprehensiveness and accuracy that
none of our American writers surpasses. It is per-

haps in this spiritual knowledge that she excels, for
she is —

> " One in whom persuasion and belief
> Had ripened into faith, and faith become
> A passionate intuition."

All her stories are evidently from the same hand
that produced " The Gates Ajar; " she could be con-
victed of their authorship on internal evidence alone.
The conscience of the woman descended from the
Puritans, sensitive and introspective to morbidness, is
incarnate in her books.   In them all one reads the
conviction that she has a message to souls diseased or
disquieted, a message of peace and comfort, and this
message she has managed to convey through her fictions not less plainly and perhaps more effectively to
many than in her avowedly didactic books.   It is to
her praise that she has done this without any sacrifice
of artistic purpose and method.   She has never
stooped to the writing of those sermons sugar-coated
with fiction, that have brought equal discredit on two
arts, both worthy of high honor, each in its own
sphere, — the arts, namely, of story-telling and of
preaching.

III.

IT would be remarkable, indeed, if such a writer
had had nothing to say on other than religious
questions.   In a biographical dictionary of some pretensions it is said of Miss Phelps: " Most of her life
has been devoted to benevolent work in her native

town, to the advancement of women, and to temperance and kindred topics." The statement may not be
precisely accurate, yet it indicates sufficiently both the
breadth of her sympathies and the practical form in
which they have been manifested. She has written
no great bulk of matter on temperance,
but a book of hers, " Jack the Fisherman " Philanthropy.
(1887), is one of the most impressive temperance
sermons ever preached, — all the more effective because there is no offensive attempt to point a moral.
Without constituting herself a common literary scold,
her pen has always been at the service of any good
cause, and she has been prompt to defend the oppressed and the friendless; and if she does not actually
enjoy taking the unpopular side, at least she never
shrinks from it.

Much of this sort of writing has been done for the
newspapers. Miss Phelps has been almost as inveterate a newspaper contributor as her father, and
both have been nearly worthy of the appellation of
journalists. In years past a number of "the Independent" that did not contain an article, a A gentle-
story, or a poem from her pen was rather woman's style.
anomalous. These articles were and are invariably
timely and readable, whatever their other characteristics may be. Miss Phelps could not be her
father's daughter and write bad English, but style
is hardly a transmissible endowment, and hers is
original. One can describe it no better than by
saying that it is the proper style of a gentlewoman,

refined, reflecting thought and study without pedan-
try, occasionally sparkling with wit, oftener glowing
with gentle humor, brilliant and vivacious at times,
well-bred and urbane always. Mrs. Burnett's style
one calls charming, Miss Phelps's might be described
as interesting, — not thereby implying that the one
lacks charm or the other interest, but in each case
indicating the dominant quality.

Miss Phelps could hardly have failed to write on
the perennial " woman question," born as she was at
a time and in a society in which the emancipation of
woman was a burning question. It is noteworthy
and refreshing to mark her way of treating it, in
contrast with the method of another New England
woman of letters, " Gail Hamilton." Miss Dodge is
a writer who may be compendiously described as
" spicy." She excels in vivacity and wit. In sarcasm and invective she has hardly a peer among
American authors. She is incisive, even combative,
by nature, and thoroughly enjoys a good hot old-
fashioned controversy, and is seldom worsted in a
The woman   verbal encounter. Her championship of
question.   her sex and its cause has been aggressive, defiant, one might add blustering if she were
a man. She has produced essays by the volume on
this theme, all thoroughly enjoyable and perhaps
none of them convincing. Miss Phelps is a far less
pungent writer, — the difference is like the difference
between allspice and cayenne pepper, — and she has
made fewer formal preachments on the subject. Her

most characteristic utterances she has chosen to put in the garb of fiction, and her say on the woman question may be found in "An Old Maid's Paradise" (1879), and its sequel, "Burglars in Paradise" (1886), and "Dr. Zay" (1884). The latter story shows the more power. The author evidently holds fast by two fundamental principles. The first is that woman has the same right to the higher education and an independent career as man, provided she wishes it and evidences the capacity for it. The second is that for the majority of women love and marriage are predestined, and the struggle against this manifest destiny for a separate career usually ends in surrender. It is not indiscreet, one hopes, to add that the author showed her faith in this teaching by her works, when in 1889 she became the wife of Mr. Herbert D. Ward, son of the veteran editor of "The Independent." We are not informed whether Dr. Zay continued her practice after marriage, but Miss Phelps (as an author she will always be known by that name) has continued her work. There was a brief attempt at collaboration on the part of Mr. and Mrs. Ward, which produced "The Master of the Magicians" (1890), and "Come Forth" (1891). This experiment can hardly be called happy, and probably the authors themselves have so concluded, for their recent work has been done independently. A successful literary partnership is one of the rarest things in literature.

IV.

THE industry of Miss Phelps — she is the author
of more than thirty volumes, the first of which was
published in 1864, which is an average of more than
a volume a year — would be remarkable in any case,
but is astonishing in the case of one who has had to
contend with ill-health, irritable nerves, and insomnia.
She has never made any plaint, never asked for public sympathy, or made a claim for kinder
Industry.   judgment on this score, but has gone on
quietly with her work. It is impossible not to admire this self-respecting reticence, and the indomi-
table will that has made so much of achievement
possible. The fact would not have been referred
to at all, in spite of its having become public prop-
erty long ago, but that it affords a clue to the better
understanding of her work. There is in her books
not a trace of the morbidness that sometimes accom-
panies a state of partial invalidism, but it is not fanciful to ascribe to that source a deep thoughtfulness, a
spiritual fervor akin to mysticism, a rapt assurance of
faith that only those know who have been made to
pass through deep waters, and have lived much alone
with themselves and God.

If there is a touch of melancholy in any of Miss
Phelps's writings it is in her verse. Two volumes
have been issued: "Poetic Studies" (1875), and
"Songs of the Silent World" (1884). It is, per-

haps, not quite just to speak of any of these verses as melancholy; the themes are generally solemn, occasionally sombre, but the treatment of them is not gloomy. The verse is stately, sober, intense, but not frigid. There is a tone of religious fervor, of unswerving faith and hope, that redeems all her poems from dismalness. Those who glance through these volumes for the first time will per- haps be surprised at finding so large a proportion of amatory verse. They might, indeed, be entitled "Poems of Passion" if that would not provoke comparison with another collection of verse bearing that title. The passion in these poems is of the genuine kind, strong, sincere, thrilling, not simulated and theatrical. It does not demand for its expression language that borders on indecency, but flows —

Her verse.

> "In numbers warmly pure and sweetly strong."

The substance of her verse is so solid, her workmanship is so conscientious always and so exquisite frequently, that Miss Phelps should be better known as a poet. And yet, if intelligent readers were asked to make a list of living American poets probably few of the lists would contain the name of Miss Phelps. This is presumably due largely to the character of the subjects she has chosen to treat, to the prevailing religious tone of her verse, and to the almost total absence of playfulness, of wit and humor, and of that *lilt* that catches the popular ear and gains

currency for work otherwise very indifferent. Her
poems are of a kind that only the cultivated, the
thoughtful, the Christian reader, can fully comprehend, and this necessarily implies a limited audience.

Of all our American women of letters Miss Phelps
impresses one as the most intense, the most high-
purposed, the most conscientious in her art. Literature is with her something more dignified than a
means of livelihood, or a path to fame; it is the high
calling of God to glorify him and to serve her fellow-
man. She is entitled to the praise of having faithfully tried to fulfil this noble ideal. The world is not
worse, but better, for every line she has written.

XII.

ADELINE D. T. WHITNEY.

FEW writers of stories have a larger circle of admirers than Mrs. Whitney, and though her books are chiefly about young people and for young people, she has found no lack of appreciative readers among adults. There is in her books, in truth, a knowledge of men and women, a philosophy of life, a humor, that cannot be fully appreciated by immature minds, though they may feel the charm of these as well as be fascinated by other qualities that lie closer to the surface. Much as she has written, there is very little to be found in the way of criticism of Mrs. Whitney's work, apart from ephemeral and usually rather perfunctory notices in newspapers and periodicals of her books as they have appeared. The appearance of a new uniform edition of her writings, in the tasteful style for which the Riverside Press is justly famous, offered a favorable opportunity for a critical study of their contents. A somewhat formidable row they make, these seventeen volumes gowned in green, witnessing to the writer's diligence and putting that of the critic to a considerable test, unless he happen to have read most of them before.

Her " complete " works.

I.

ADELINE DUTTON TRAIN is a native of Boston, and spent her early life in that city. Her father, Enoch Train, was a successful man of business, the founder of a line of packet-ships between Boston and Liverpool, in the palmy days when the American clipper was the queen of the seas. The brilliant, eccentric, erratic George Francis Train is her brother. The vein of mysticism in the writings of the sister has cropped out into something very like insanity in the brother, but the native mental gifts of both were far above the common and also out of the common.

A brief biography.

No doubt some of Mrs. Whitney's stories contain a large element of autobiography, but only she and her nearest friends could tell where history ends and fiction begins in her Faith Gartneys and Leslie Goldthwaites. It would be perilous to attempt disentangling the two during her lifetime; but in after years the " higher critic " may disport himself in reconstructing the story of her girlhood from the internal evidence afforded by her writings. What we now know certainly is, that before her girlhood was well passed, at the age of nineteen in fact, Miss Train became the wife of Seth D. Whitney, of Milton, Mass., and has lived a quiet home life in that town ever since. Mrs. Whitney has, it would appear, studiously avoided putting her personality in evidence before the public. She has virtually said, "My books belong to the world, my life belongs to myself, my family, my friends." It is the duty of the critic to respect this reticence, and to inquire no further into the personality of the writer than the writings themselves fairly warrant one in going. What of herself she has put into print is ours to know and to discuss. The rest belongs to the privacy of a gentlewoman, that nobody has a right to invade.

II.

AT the very outset one is tempted to break one's good resolution not to go behind the facts of record, because the first fact arouses a curiosity that is not altogether impertinent. Mrs. Whitney's first recorded publication is a poem, "Footsteps on the Seas" (Boston, 1857). As she has per- Began as a poet. mitted the date of her birth to become part of her public record, it cannot be indiscreet to remark that the writer of this poem was already in her thirties, and to add that most of our American men and women of letters have shown the symptoms of the pen-and-ink disease at a much earlier period. Hence one's curiosity: did Mrs. Whitney have literary ambitions, and do the usual preparatory scribbling in her early years; or did she (as we know was the case with "H. H.") make her first real essays in literature after she had reached middle life? This first publication of Mrs. Whitney's, few of her admirers have

ever seen, and it is not included in this last edition
of her works, from which one might be justified in
inferring a fixed intention to disown this bantling,
were not four other volumes of her verses also
omitted.

The second book published by her still holds the
field, " Mother Goose for Grown Folks" (New York,
1860), and is deservedly a favorite with all her
readers. In a revised, enlarged, and glorified form
—illustrated, that is to say, by Augustus Hoppin—
it has a place in the latest edition of her
writings. It is really a very clever book. *Mother Goose.*
In the main aspiring to be nothing more than a *jeu
d'esprit*, not professing to possess high poetic merit,
and somewhat careless as to workmanship, its playfulness and wit mask a good deal of serious purpose.
For example, these stanzas suggested by the familiar
" Rockaby baby": —

> " O golden gift of childhood!
>   That, with its kingly touch,
>   Transforms to more than royalty
>   The thing it loveth much!
>   O second sight, bestowed alone
>   Upon the baby seer,
>   That the glory held in Heaven's reserve
>   Discerneth even here!
>
>   .   .   .   .   .   .
>
> " O golden gift of childhood!
>   If the talisman might last,
>   How dull the Present still should gleam
>   With the glory of the Past.

> But the things of earth about us
> Fade and dwindle as we go,
> And the long perspective of our life
> Is truth, and not a show!"

Very amusing is "Brahmic," her parody on Emerson's celebrated "Brahma," which she ingeniously turns into praise of Mother Goose: —

> "If a great poet think he sings,
>   Or if the poem think it's sung,
> They do but sport the scattered plumes
>   That Mother Goose aside hath flung.

> "Far or forgot to me is near:
>   Shakespeare and Punch are all the same;
> The vanished thoughts do reappear,
>   And shape themselves to fun or fame."

In later years Mrs. Whitney has published four small collections of verse: "Pansies" (1872), "Holytides" (1886), and "Bird Talk" and "Daffodils" (1887). None of these is included in the present collection of her writings. Of her verse as a whole, it is not unjust to say that the public is right in not esteeming it as her chief title to fame. It shows talents that, devoted exclusively to this kind of composition, might have given her high rank among the poets of America, since the conception of her poems is usually much above the formal embodiment of it. Most of her verse is contemplative, religious, with a tinge of mysticism. Her tendency is to see the hidden meaning, not in some things, but in everything —

> " As the Swedish seer contends,
> All things comprise an inner sense."

This, which doubtless constitutes the charm of her verses to readers like-minded, is rather a bar to the appreciation of them by the many.

III.

IT was not until the publication of " Boys at Chequasset," in 1862, that Mrs. Whitney really found her vocation.   She has done much better work since, but *Finding her vocation.* that story is still as fresh and pleasing as when it was written.   Her portrait of " Johnnie," the careless, slovenly, hurry-scurry boy, is true to the life, and the process of his reformation is ingeniously worked out, without too great a draft on one's credulity or the making of him into a hateful prig.   Five books then followed in quick succession, of which to this day many of the author's readers do not know which is their favorite: "Faith Gartney's Girlhood" (1863); "The Gayworthys" (1865); "A Summer in Leslie Goldthwaite's Life" (1866); " Patience Strong's Outings " (1868); and " Hitherto " (1869).   Mrs. Whitney may have done as good work since, — opinions might conceivably differ as to that, — but probably nobody will affirm that she has done better work than in these five stories.   They mark the summit of her achievement in fiction, and by them the quality and value of that achievement may be fairly tested.

The first and most vivid impression made by these books is that their author knows how to tell a story. This is not so common a faculty as might be supposed. Some of the greatest novelists have lacked it. Some have been destitute of it altogether, and are great nevertheless, but their ad- A story-teller. mirers are comparatively few. A writer with something of Scott's gift of story-telling can win the hearts of his readers though he fail in pretty much everything else, while one who has this talent in small measure must have shining gifts indeed to compensate for its absence. Mrs. Whitney gets the reader's attention at the outset and holds it by the interest of her story. But this is by no means her only hold on the reader; she has the power of characterization, of making us believe in the solid reality of the personages with whom she peoples her books. Scott's books are fascinating for their stories, but could anything be more shadowy and unsubstantial than his Ivanhoes and Quentin Durwards, his Peverils and Guy Mannerings? Who ever thinks of them as he thinks of Falstaff and Hamlet, and in a less degree of Faith Gartney and Patience Strong? Mrs. Whitney's readers have been known to hold long discussions regarding the people of her stories, in which their actions and characters were canvassed and compared, and such discussions sometimes have waxed warm. People do not work themselves into a state of high moral indignation over personages of a novel, unless the author has a large measure of creative power, and so makes her pen-and-ink men and women as real as flesh and blood to her readers.

The power of these books is largely due to their style. How Mrs. Whitney might write if she attempted something in prose outside of fiction, one can only guess. In that case her work might or might not deserve to be commended for its literary graces. The quality of her style that gives it savor and effec-
Her homely tiveness in her stories is its homeliness.
style. She does not disdain the vocabulary of ordinary every-day life, the English that New England people use when they are not trying to be elegant and to " speak good grammar." She writes as simply, unaffectedly, and directly as people talk, and this naturalness goes a long way towards not merely explaining but justifying her popularity. Her young readers feel the value of this quality without being sufficiently analytic to tell what it is; and her older readers, enjoying it more understandingly, know it to be a gift that only a few American writers possess. The bane of modern literature is self-consciousness and affectation; if Mrs. Whitney's unconsciousness of self is the result of study and labor, she has indeed mastered that last secret of art, apparent artlessness.

Lively sallies of wit are not so common in these stories as that quiet, rather dry humor, born of native
Humor. shrewdness and close observation, which distinguishes the Yankee. Emery Ann is nearly as keen as the more famous Mrs. Poyser,

and a good deal more droll; and there are other characters nearly her equal. She lacks the poetic insight, the touch of genius, that Mr. Lowell has infused into Hosea Biglow, but in other traits she is his literary twin-sister. Genuine humor is a rare quality in women who write novels, and one ought to be proportionately grateful when he finds it so plentiful and of so high quality as in Mrs. Whitney's books.

This leaves for mention at the very last, what many would put first of all, the religious tone of these and other stories by Mrs. Whitney. Some readers do not value this part of her work so highly, for several reasons. One is that the writer too often makes her books and even her characters "preachy." This is always bad art, but it is also bad from the moralist's point of view, because it is comparatively ineffective. The only moral worth inculcating in a work of fiction is one that does not need to be inculcated, — the impression that the simple telling of the story, the mere working out of character, the unavoidable results of wrong-doing and the equally certain reward of goodness, make upon the reader without the author's comment. It is only the crude beginner in art who needs to put beneath his picture, "This is a horse," and there is something wrong about a story if its moral must be impressed on the reader by little preachments, whether the author's own or put into the mouths of her characters. Many sayings in Mrs. Whitney's books that

Religious tone.

would be admirable in a book of moral maxims, or in a collection of religious meditations, are better fitted to provoke the scoffer than to comfort and strengthen the saint, in their present location.

Another fact that lessens the appreciation of some for the religious element of these stories has already been mentioned in another connection, — their fre-

Her mysti-cism. quent, not to say prevailing, tone of mysticism. The trail of Emanuel Swedenborg is over them all. Swedenborg is the one great religious writer — one calls him great in deference to the opinions of others — from whom many would confess without shame that they have never been able to extract the least profit, and barely the semblance of an idea. It is difficult to have patience with anybody who pretends to understand him, or to extract profound truths from his chaos of words. His mysticism seems only one degree more intellectually respectable than theosophy. There are multitudes of readers of Mrs. Whitney in such case. It may argue a defect of mind or of soul in them that they are unable to see the thing that is not, — let us grant this to be the case; but because of this defect they cannot find in a considerable part of Mrs. Whitney's religious teachings the comfort and inspiration that some profess to derive from them.

Mrs. Whitney's books for many years showed a growing artistic power. The "preachy" tone she

outgrew in good part, and with experience in authorship her touch became more sure, her mastery of her
materials more complete.   Her last books, A growing
if they have not greatly surpassed the power.
others, have at least shown no waning of her powers;
and in some of them she has shown her ability to
write about and for others than young people.   Pre-
dictions regarding the future rank of the authors of
our own day are about as valuable as the "oldest
inhabitant's" confident remarks about to-morrow's
weather, but there seems to be no good reason to
question that Mrs. Whitney's books will continue to
instruct and delight more than one generation of
Americans after all her present readers are gathered
to their fathers.

XIII.

BRET HARTE.

NOTHING in the history of this Western world is more romantic than the story of California. Though it was early settled by Spaniards, it had little part in the life of this continent, until the revolutionary action of "The Pathfinder" secured its addition to the Union. Even then its develop-

The Argonauts of '49. ment would have been slow, in the natural course of events, but events did not take their natural course. The discovery of gold precipitated upon the Pacific coast a horde of adventurous spirits, and California advanced by great leaps towards civilization and Statehood. In a single generation the work of centuries was accomplished. Cities sprang up as if built by the slaves of Aladdin's lamp. Forests were hewn down, and what forests! Vast engineering enter-prises were undertaken and accomplished; railways were built, mountains were tunnelled, rivers were bridged, streams were turned from their beds to do the bidding of man. Those who made this new commonwealth out of a wilderness were no weak-lings. The difficulties of the overland trail and of the Cape Horn voyage produced a natural selection of the fittest. As their best historian tells us: "The faith, courage, vigor, youth, and capacity for adventure necessary to this emigration produced a body of men as strongly distinctive as the companions of Jason. Unlike most pioneers, the majority were men of profession and education; all were young, and all had staked their fortune in the enterprise. . . . Eastern magazines and current Eastern literature formed their literary recreation, and the sale of the better class of periodicals was singularly great. . . . The author records that he has experienced more difficulty in procuring a copy of 'Punch' in an English provincial town than was his fortune at 'Red Dog' or 'One-Horse Gulch.'"

Thrown upon their own resources altogether, separated by almost the breadth of a continent from civilization, these new-comers rapidly developed social and moral standards of their own, improvised laws for their government, and executed these laws with such celerity, impartiality, and substantial equity as civilized jurisprudence may envy but can hardly hope to surpass. Though the majority of these Argonauts were men of education and conscience, there was a strong sprinkling of the vicious, the degraded, the criminal classes among them. Freed from artificial restraints, and from the softening influences of womankind, the natural man showed himself in this pioneer life, and made of it something wilder,

A picturesque era.

more picturesque, more individual in flavor than
has been known elsewhere on this continent, — the
like of which has, indeed, seldom been seen anywhere. It was altogether fitting that this pioneer
life, with its vices and its virtues, should be em-
balmed in literature; and the man for the times
was found in a young printer of San Francisco.

I.

FRANCIS BRET HARTE — he has of late years
dropped the first of these names, presumably given
Birth and boy- him by his sponsors in baptism — was
hood.   born in Albany, August 25, 1839. His
father was a teacher in the Female Seminary of
that city, which was then one of the noted schools
of the State. He was a man of culture and taste,
but died when his son was a mere lad, leaving his
family unprovided for. Why his widow should
have gone to California in 1854 is not recorded,
and such a course on her part baffles conjecture;
but go she did, and the youthful Bret went with
her, to his own ultimate good fortune, and the
greater fortune of American literature. The boy,
under these circumstances, was unusually lucky
to get even the common-school education that we
are assured he received; and at no advanced age,
we may be sure, he was compelled to look out for
himself. His first experiment in this line is said
to have been in his father's footsteps; he walked

from San Francisco to Sonora and opened a school. This enterprise was unsuccessful, — not, we may be sure, owing to lack of push and zeal in the teacher, — and he next turned his attention to mining. Failing in this also, he thereupon obtained employment in a printing-office and became a compositor.

From type-setting to literature is but a short step, and Bret Harte was not long in taking it. In a lately printed newspaper "interview" he has told us of a still earlier literary venture of his, — a poem called "Autumn Musings." He remarks that "it was written at the mature age of eleven. It was satirical in character, and cast upon the fading year the cynical light of my repressed dis- First attempt satisfaction with things in general. I at writing. addressed the envelope to the 'New York Sunday Atlas,' at that time a journal of some literary repute in New York, where I was then living.

"I was not quite certain how the family would regard this venture on my part, and I posted the missive with the utmost secrecy. After that I waited for over a week in a state of suspense that entirely absorbed me. Sunday came, and with it the newspapers. These were displayed on a stand on the street near our house, and held in their places — I shall never forget them — with stones. With an unmoved face, but a beating heart, I scanned the topmost copy of the 'Atlas.' To my dying day I shall remember the thrill that came from seeing 'Autumn Musings,' a poem, on the first page. I don't know that the headline type was any larger than usual, but to me it was colossal. It had something of the tremendousness of a three-sheet poster. I bought the paper and took it home. I exhibited it to the family by slow and cautious stages. My hopes sank lower and lower. At last I realized the enormity of my offence. The lamentation was general. It was unanimously conceded that I was lost, and I fully believed it. My idea of a poet — it was the family's idea also — was the Hogarthian one, born of a book of Hogarth's drawings belonging to my father. In the lean and miserable and helpless guise of 'The Distressed Poet,' as therein pictured, I saw, aided by the family, my probable future. It was a terrible experience. I sometimes wonder that I ever wrote another line of verse."

Budding genius is not to be so lightly repressed, however, and Harte had not set type long before he had aspirations after the higher walks of journalism. His first articles were composed at the case, without the intervention of a manuscript, and these contributions apparently found favor with his superiors, for during the absence of the editor he was somewhat rashly put in charge of the paper. The subscribers were largely miners, and some of the young editor's squibs so seriously offended them that there was a hasty return of the editor and an abrupt termination of the young man's editorial experience. He had however, found his vocation, though, for a time, he was himself but half-conscious of the fact.

II.

DRIFTING back to San Francisco, Mr. Harte found employment as a compositor on the " Golden Era." A young author who has once seen himself in print, is no more to be restrained from gratify- From "case" ing his passion than a young tiger who to desk. has for the first time tasted blood. There began to appear in the " Golden Era" anonymous sketches of frontier and mining life, and the conductors of the paper were not long in making inquiries about their authorship. When the young type-setter was discovered to be the guilty man, he was invited to lay down his "stick" and take up the pen. His editorial experience here was not long, however, for we find him soon after in charge of a literary weekly, called the " San Francisco Californian." It was in this paper that his clever " Condensed Novels" first made their appearance.

However cultivated Californians may have been in the sixties, and however well they may have patronized the literary periodicals of the East, and even of Europe, they do not appear to have appreciated their home product. " The Californian" lived for a time at a poor dying rate, and at length ceased to live at all. Mr. Harte then secured, in 1864, an appointment as secretary of the United

States Mint in San Francisco, a post that he continued to hold for six years, with satisfaction to
himself and his superior officers.   His duties were
not so onerous that he was unable to continue his
literary labors; on the contrary, he wrote steadily,
if not profusely, and laid the foundations
Writes poems.
of his reputation as a poet.   "John Burns
of Gettysburg," justly esteemed one of his best
poems, belongs to this period; so does "The Society
upon the Stanislaus," one of the best known and
most frequently quoted of his humorous poems.
There are few, even of those inveterate newspaper
readers that seldom look into a book, who have not
heard of the animated debate provoked in that grave
society by Mr. Brown's discovery of some fossil
bones, or the sad fate of one man, when—

> " A chunk of old red sandstone took him in the abdomen,
> And he smiled a kind of sickly smile, and curled up on the
>   floor,
> And the subsequent proceedings interested him no more."

These poems were first published in the San Francisco newspapers, but they caught the public fancy
and were widely copied, giving the author his first
taste of a continental fame.

It is a curious fact, and one on which Mr. Harte
himself dwells with bitter philosophy, that his
efforts to portray the pioneer life that he
Without honor
in his own
country.   knew so well, whether in prose or verse,
met with little local reward.   Of reward in the
shape of hard cash, we are justified in believing

that they received nothing at all. Of praise they
received only just enough to keep the author from
throwing down his pen in despair. The educated
men of California had been trained in a different
school of literature; their taste had been formed on
the English and American classics. Shakespeare
they knew, and Wordsworth, and Bryant, and Poe,
but who was this upstart, with his mixture of local
slang and queer morals, to deserve their admiration?
Once more a prophet had appeared to make good
the ancient saying; and it was not until the plaudits
of the cultured East greeted Bret Harte as the
rising star of a new literature that he found honor
in his own country. By that time he had shaken
the dust of California from his feet forever.

This is, however, to anticipate our story somewhat. In July, 1868, was begun the publication of
"The Overland Monthly," a somewhat
ambitious periodical that aspired to be   An editor.
for the Pacific coast what "The Atlantic Monthly"
had become for the East. Mr. Harte had so far
established his reputation that he was indicated to
the publisher as the best man to conduct the editorial part of the new enterprise. It seemed to the
editor to be a defect in the first number published
that it contained no romance distinctively Californian; and accordingly he set himself to work to
remedy the defect. "The Luck of Roaring Camp"
was the result of his labors. Having sent the
manuscript to the printer, the editor-author was

fairly entitled to consider his work ended, but it
turned out to be just begun.   One who reads the
story now can hardly credit the account of the row
that was raised over its publication.   The trouble
was begun by the proof-reader, and the printer took
the extraordinary course of returning the proofs,
not to the editor, but to the publisher, with the
emphatic declaration that the matter was "so indecent, irreligious, and improper," that his reader
(a young woman) had with difficulty been induced
to continue its perusal.   One can hardly credit,
also, that such a characterization of the story
received the least attention from the publisher,
still less that it produced an acute editorial crisis.
Such, however, we are assured by Mr. Harte, was
the fact.   Ultimately the publisher decided to stand
by the literary judgment of his editor, and not to
have his magazine edited by the printer and proof-
reader, but it was with fear and trembling that he
saw the number go out.   Its reception in California
must have confirmed his worst misgivings, but the
An immediate   verdict of the East was different.   The
success.   return mail brought a letter to the author
from the publishers of the "Atlantic Monthly,"
requesting, on the most flattering terms, a story for
that magazine similar to "The Luck of Roaring
Camp."   Mr. Harte tells us that when he placed
this letter in the hands of his publisher, he felt his
compensation to be complete.   He had caught the
ear of the public at last.   He had discovered the

vein that he could profitably spend the rest of his
life in working.

From this time, during the brief continuance of
his California life, stories and poems flowed rapidly
from Bret Harte's pen. "The Outcasts of Poker
Flat" deepened the impression made by his first
tale, and is considered by many to be his finest
story. "Miggles," "Tennessee's Partner," and
other stories came in quick succession, and the
crowning touch was given to his popularity by
the appearance in the number of the "Overland
Monthly" for September, 1870, of "Plain Language
from Truthful James," the well-known The "Heathen
verses about Ah Sin, the Heathen Chinee. Chinee."
This poem is of slight literary value, compared
with some of Mr. Harte's other work in verse, but
it is a clever skit enough, and it happened to appear
just at the time to meet with the heartiest welcome.
Lines and phrases of it became household words all
over the United States, and in spite of being now
familiar even to triteness, they are still quoted by
newspapers and public speakers as the word most
pat to the occasion when John Chinaman is discussed. The satire of the poem exposed better,
perhaps, than sober argument could, the shallowness of the grounds on which the cry, "The Chinese
must go," was raised. One questions whether some
of the author's unpopularity in California may not
be due to this championship of oppressed and mal-
treated John.

III.

In the year following the publication of this poem Bret Harte left California, and has never
Leaves California. returned.   He had won a public for himself, but not on the Pacific Coast; there his recognition was slight from the first, and is still anything but general or fervid.   Even now there are Californians who assert very positively that Bret Harte is not a representative Californian writer; that he has resided so long abroad as to lose his connection with the State, and that his books portray a condition of society that has long ceased to exist.   Something very like antipathy is felt towards him now on the Pacific coast, instead of the cold indifference with which his first work was received there.   Before he left, however, he had won recognition of a certain sort from those who were qualified to appreciate good work, as is shown by the fact that in 1870 he was appointed Professor of Recent Literature in the University of California.   It does not appear that he ever did any work in connection with this chair, and he could not have held it more than a single year, for in 1871 he came to New York.

It was a somewhat Bohemian existence that he led in the metropolis, with no certain source of income and no regular occupation.   There was at one time some talk of founding a literary periodical in Chicago to be conducted by him, but the capital apparently was not forthcoming; at any rate, nothing came of it. He continued *Bohemianism.* to contribute stories to the "Atlantic Monthly," and, we believe, made pot-boilers for New York journals; but perhaps his best known work of this period was his lecture on "The Argonauts of '49." This lecture was delivered in many places, and must have been a considerable pecuniary success; but Mr. Harte failed to make a deep impression on the lecture-hearing public and gained no permanent place in the lyceum field. This was perhaps as well for him. Had he been gifted with elocutionary graces that win the favor of ordinary audiences he might have been tempted from his legitimate work.

It was in 1878 that he left his native country, practically for good, for though he may have made a brief visit or two since then, he has *Goes abroad.* resided most of the time abroad. He was first appointed consul to Crefeld, Germany, by President Hayes, and in 1880 was transferred to Glasgow. In this latter place he remained until a change of administration in 1885 and the exigencies of politics compelled his retirement. Since that time he has lived for the most part in London. He is a favorite in English society, and appears definitely to have joined that small but select body of Americans who for one reason or another have voluntarily expatriated themselves. From the time of his going abroad to the present moment there is little to tell about him, except the titles of the books he has published. These have been quite numerous, and all in the same vein with his "Luck of Roaring Camp" and other early tales. They merely repeat and amplify the picture of life and manners that he drew for us in that first volume. The most indulgent critic can say no more of these later volumes than that they are not unworthy of what he published before 1870.

IV.

BRET HARTE is a singular example of the force that lies in narrowness. Speaking broadly, he is

Narrowness. able to do just one thing well, and that is to delineate the life with which he became familiar in his early days. He can do that only in one way, through the medium of the short story. No, that is not just; he can also do it through the dialect ballad. There is no better work of the kind than "Dow's Flat" and other poems of a similar tone that he wrote late in the sixties. But in recent years he seems to have abandoned verse as medium of expression, and confined himself to prose. He has also, with a single exception, confined himself to the short story in his fictions. His "Gabriel Conroy" (Hartford, 1876), the one case in which he attempted a full-grown novel, was something very like a failure, —

as near as a man of genius can come to failure
when he attempts something beyond his powers.
He was convinced by that experiment that his forte
was in another direction, and has had the practical
good sense to heed the lesson. This is not a
common thing among authors, who seem to have
the same kind of fondness for the works condemned
by the world that a mother has for a deformed or
feeble-minded child. Milton thought his "Paradise Regained" superior to his "Paradise Lost;"
Bunyan could never see that the second *Perversity*
part of "The Pilgrim's Progress" was *of authors.*
unequal to the first; and of all his poems Tennyson
considered "Maud" the best. Tennyson affords an
even more melancholy instance of wilfulness in his
persistent writing of dramatic works, the best of
which is not above second or third class. Mr.
Harte is therefore to be credited with unusual
intelligence in the perception of what he could do
best, and uncommon self-control in restricting himself to that kind of work. There is an advantage
not to be lightly esteemed in thus restricting one's
sphere. Breadth is very well when it does not
mean shallowness, but with narrowness commonly
goes a certain depth and force. None of our
American writers has been narrower in range
than Hawthorne and Poe, and of all our writers
they are the most intense.

Much objection has been raised to some of Bret
Harte's stories on the ground of their supposed

immoral tendency. It must be admitted by his most ardent admirers that he decidedly prefers as Alleged immo- heroes and heroines of his tales people rality. of shady antecedents, — social outcasts preferred, but anybody who is in the habit of daily shattering a few of the commandments will answer his purpose. It is a remarkable fact, however, that the depravity of his characters is little more than skin deep; the worst of them are capable on occasion of transcendent deeds of heroism and self-sacrifice. His villains are, in truth, not very villanous, for their failings have a strong leaning to virtue's side. One suspects that their wicked-ness is only a quality imputed to them by the author to make them more interesting. It must be confessed that he has some justification for this course. Simple goodness, as material for fiction, is not very available; it is so often simple dulness. After all, from the strict moralist's point of view there can be no objection to the villain in fiction *per se*, else he must condemn "Paradise Lost" and "Othello" as immoral works. It is the moral lesson that the author teaches which justifies or condemns his choice of a villain as a hero. Bret Harte makes a spirited, and, one must think, a conclusive reply to the charge of immorality made His reply. against him on the ground that he has shown too much mercy to the wicked: "When it shall be proven to him that communities are degraded and brought to guilt and crime, suffering or destitution, from a predominance of this quality; when he shall see pardoned ticket-of-leave men elbowing men of austere lives out of situation and position, and the repentant Magdalen supplanting the blameless virgin in society, then he will lay aside his pen and extend his hand to the new Draconian discipline in fiction. But until then he will, without claiming to be a religious man or a moralist, but simply as an artist, reverently and humbly conform to the rules laid down by a Great Poet, who created the parable of the 'Prodigal Son' and the 'Good Samaritan,' whose works have lasted eighteen hundred years, and will remain when the present writer and his generation are forgotten."

The real objection to Bret Harte's stories does not rest on moral, but on artistic grounds. The trouble with his villains is not that they The real objection. are too bad, but that they are not bad enough, — that is to say, they are not real. Such villains never were on sea or land outside of his stories, unless we except the Bowery stage in the melodrama of "ye olden time." There is a glare of the footlights, an atmosphere of the theatre, about too many of these tales, — not the best of them, for the best work of Mr. Harte is free from this defect, and ranks among the choicest in recent American literature. Another artistic defect in these tales is that their sentiment does not ring true; it often flats into sentimentality. More than any of our other American writers of fiction, Mr.

Harte is a disciple of Dickens, and he unfortunately often falls into the mawkishness of his master. He does not attempt the tender-pathetic with any "Little Nells" and "Paul Dombeys," but he preaches to satiety the duty of charity to the publican and the sinner. We tire of it, precisely as we tire of the sentimental gush of Dickens about Christmas, and for the same reason, — not merely that there is too much of it, but that it does not seem to be quite the genuine thing.

In his verse Bret Harte has shown a somewhat wider range. He does to perfection the humorous dialect rhymes in which his favorite Californians figure, but he strikes other and higher keys. Of these his "John Burns," as already noted, is one fine example, and others are "Dickens in Camp," "Twenty Years," "Telemachus and his Mentor," "Half an Hour before Supper," "To the Pliocene Skull," and "Mrs. Judge Jenkins." Each of these represents a different manner, and each is of high excellence in its way. Had Mr. Harte been able to devote himself more exclusively to verse, one is warranted in believing that his name would have ranked high among American poets.

It is a fact not to be passed by, that Bret Harte is one of the few American authors whose popu-

Popularity abroad. larity is even greater abroad than at home. Our English kin have a standard of literary excellence much like our own, but they have also an ideal peculiar to themselves of what is or should be American, and they are very exacting critics in this regard. They will not admit anything to be distinctively American unless it has some flavor of wildness, some garb of uncouthness. It is the same tendency of mind that makes the cockney tourist look about the streets of New York for the aborigines in paint and feathers that he has taught himself to expect, and to be vastly surprised at being told that he cannot hunt buffaloes and other big game in the immediate vicinity of our great cities. It is the good fortune of Bret Harte and one or two other American writers to have profited by this peculiarity of the reading Briton. Nobody will envy him his good fortune. One could wish, however, that the Briton might learn to admire, not with less of heartiness, but with more of intelligent discrimination, the literary work of the American Cousin.

XIV.

EDWARD EVERETT HALE.

VERSATILITY is too common a trait in Americans to be regarded as characteristic of any individual, and American men of letters are by no means lacking in this national idiosyncrasy. There is here and there one among the knights of the quill, nevertheless, who realizes so fully the traditional accomplishments of the admirable Crichton as to become a constant wonder to his brother workers and a positive marvel to the

Versatility. general. Reaching supreme excellence in no one thing, perhaps, but only just missing it in several things, and doing half a score as only the picked men of his generation can do them, — if there were an "all around" championship in literature as there is in athletics it would surely fall to a man of this type. Such a man was Lowell; such a man was Oliver Wendell Holmes; but perhaps of all the American writers of our day the one who excels in this "all around" work is Edward Everett Hale. He has raised versatility to the nth power, and covered with ignominy the hoary old proverb, for while he might be called a Jack at all trades, he is master of all. *Nihil tetigit*

— the saying is something musty, but as applied to him its truth redeems it from triteness and gives it fresh currency. He has done much to give the world innocent amusement; he has done even more to make the world better.

I.

SOME witty but not very reverent American has remarked that a man who is fortunate enough to be born in Boston does not need to be born again. This felicity was Mr. Hale's in .1822. His ancestry was no less fortunate than his birthplace. The founder of the family was the Rev. John Hale, a divine of some repute in the Salem witchcraft days. The reverend John was a believer in witchcraft at the first, as we learn from his treatise, "A Modest Inquiry into the Nature of Witchcraft," published in 1697, but he afterwards came to a more rational view of the matter. Curiously enough, he was the only minister in the family for several generations, — all his descendants becoming either physicians or journalists. The literary bent in the family has always been strong, especially so in the immediate family of Dr. Hale. The father was a journalist; an elder brother, Nathan, followed in his footsteps; and a sister, Lucretia P., is a well-known writer for the magazines and author of books. They all took to literature as naturally as if ink and not blood was the

circulating fluid in their veins.   Of his early Boston
days Dr. Hale has lately given us a series of very
interesting reminiscences, called "Recollections of
a New England Boyhood."   The book lacks the humor of Warner and Aldrich, and the keen observation of Howells, but it supplements their boyhood
autobiographies very pleasantly.

Dr. Hale's education was gained in the Boston
Latin School and at Harvard College, where he
Education.   was graduated in 1839.   The next two
years were spent in teaching and the
study of theology, and in 1842 he was licensed.
For several years he did not have a settled charge,
but preached in various Unitarian churches.   In
1846 he was pastor at Worcester, but the settlement
was a brief one, for the following year he received
a call from the South Congregational church, of
Boston.   This church, one notes by the way, has
never abandoned its orthodox name, though it gave
up its orthodox faith early in the great Unitarian
defection.   Here for nearly half a century he has
been the conscientious and hard-working pastor of
a great city parish, and his pulpit has been a
recognized force in the religious life of Boston
during all those years.

Dr. Hale is so much better known to the general
public as a man of letters than as a Christian min-
Preacher.   ister, one may be pardoned for dwelling
a little on this feature of his work.   He
is not a theologian.   By that one does not mean

that he may not be learned in the history of dogma, and well versed in current theological speculation, or even an original thinker on the great problems of religion, but merely that he has not chosen to give the results of his study and thought to the world in formal theological treatises. He is not a great pulpit orator. There was a time when no visitor to the metropolis was thought to have seen the great show properly until he "went to hear Beecher." Dr. Hale has never been a part of Boston's show in that way. There have been sensationalists like the late "Adirondack" Murray, and genuine Christian preachers like Phillips Brooks, who have been more prominent in the public prints and have caught the popular ear more successfully, but this sort of popularity is no real measure of a preacher's influence. Dr. Hale, without being a great orator, is a preacher of originality, freshness, pungency, practicality. Moreover, he does not preach negations, he does not engage in dialectic duels with orthodoxy or agnosticism, but faithfully preaches the positive truth as he understands it. He does not preach morals, he preaches religion. And therefore, while there have been other men, now this one and now that, who have temporarily seemed to have more vogue with the people of Boston than he, there has been no more powerful and constant religious force in that city during the past half century than the pulpit of the South Church.

Nor has he been a preacher and writer so exclusively as to seclude himself from his people and hold himself exempt from the duties of a pastor. He has faithfully shepherded the flock. There has been a well-trodden path between his study door and the homes of his people, and none have gone to him in vain for sympathy, for consolation, for help. He has not frittered away his time in making social, gossipy calls on his parishioners, which is the ideal of pastoral visitation that widely obtains among both ministers and laymen, but he has not spared his time or strength wherever he could be of real service in ministering to the sick or the afflicted. In his case charity has begun at home, though it has not ended there.

Pastor.

II.

DR. HALE first won public recognition as a man of letters through the "Atlantic Monthly." In one of the early numbers of that magazine his " My Double, and How he Undid me " almost immediately became widely known and highly appreciated. This success was repeated and intensified by other contributions to the same periodical, that placed him at once in the front rank of story-writers. The most famous of these stories, of course, is " The Man Without a Country," and it strikingly illustrates the author's chief characteristic as a story-writer. This is a power, such

Philip Nolan.

as perhaps no writer since Defoe has so fully possessed, of surrounding his tales with an atmosphere of verisimilitude. In reading many authors' stories we say, "That might have happened," but after reading Hale's stories we say, "That did happen precisely as it is written." This story of Philip Nolan, though of imagination all compact, has been believed to be historical by thousands of readers, — "thousands" is no exaggeration in this case, but rather an understatement, — and people of vivid imagination and vague ideas of veracity have even been known to assert that they had seen Philip Nolan and knew him to be no myth. Greater tribute than this to a writer's power could not well be paid.

"The Skeleton in the Closet," like "My Double," is an example of whimsical humor superadded to this gift of lifelike narration. There are Characteristics. some American humorists whose stories are very funny, but are so marked by exaggeration of traits that we feel at once, though we may not say, "Nobody could possibly be such a fool;" and there are other stories whose incidents are so absurd that they could never by any possibility have happened. But when Mr Hale tells us how a hoop-skirt destroyed the Southern Confederacy, while the fundamental idea is deliciously absurd, every link in the chain of fact he forges bears the weight of any test of credibility, — it all might have happened just so, and while we read we have no doubt that it did so happen, though, of course, we know it did n't.   In this power to invent and tell a story bearing all the marks of history, Dr. Hale is without a peer among American writers.

He is not so successful, however, in dealing with a theme that demands larger treatment.   Few

Novels less successful.
writers, indeed, are equally successful in dealing with the tale and the novel. The two species of composition demand gifts quite different and not often combined in one person. In a short story incident is everything; there can be no elaborate studies of character; everything must be sketched with a few bold strokes, and there must be no halting by the way.   In the novel, on the contrary, the effect is produced by a multitude of details; digressions from the main purpose, if not too frequent or too long, are permissible; and the study of character is far more important than incident.   Books like "Ups and Downs" and "Gone to Texas" cannot be called much more than short stories spun out so as to fill a volume.   This is merely to say, however, that even so versatile a man of letters as Dr. Hale, while he fails in nothing that he undertakes, does not reach an equal height of excellence in everything.   If his short stories were not of a quality so superlative, his novels might, perhaps, have met with a higher appreciation.   What would be brilliant success in another, we count but moderate achievement in him.

III.

As a writer of fiction, Dr. Hale has been fairly prolific, but this is only one of the departments of literature cultivated by him. If all his fictions, short and long, were blotted out, _{Historian.} he would still have a title to grateful remembrance as a writer of history. Besides being a valued contributor to many works that do not bear his name, — like Winsor's "History of Boston," — his name appears on the titlepage of some twelve historical writings. A number of these are "popular" books, the author merely taking his materials from standard works and telling the facts in an effective way. "Stories of Discovery" is a good specimen of this kind of work. In other books Dr. Hale has made original and important contributions to historic knowledge. Witness his paper before the American Antiquarian Society, in which he recounts his discovery of how the State of California received its name; also his volume of "Original Documents from the State Paper Office," in which the true history of Sir Walter Raleigh's first American colony and the colony at Jamestown was first accurately told.

Had Dr. Hale chosen to devote his energies to the writing of history, he might, without doubt, have taken rank among the greatest historians. The same faculty of life-like narration, of making men and events seem intensely real to the reader, that is so great a power in his fictions, would The histories too "popular." have been a wondrous gift in the writer of sober history. This faculty is manifest in the historical writing Dr. Hale has actually given us, but not to the degree one might wish. Indeed, though it seems ungracious to say it, these historical books are less satisfactory to one who studies them critically than the author's other writings. They are unsatisfactory mainly because they manifestly fall so far short of what he was and is capable of accomplishing. They are superficial, in many cases, in their treatment of the material. A "popular" book need not be uncritical and unscholarly; beneath the text should be solid attainment and careful study, though processes are kept out of sight and only results are given to the reader, — as the skeleton gives form and strength to the body, though invisible. Dr. Hale's "popular" books, moreover, are often as slipshod in style as they are superficial in scholarship. They betray marks of haste in composition. They are clever first drafts rather than carefully finished works. This is the penalty of the versatility so remarkable, and the industry not less remarkable, that mark the literary career of Dr. Hale. Nevertheless, when all possible deductions are made, there are but one or two living historians who might not have been proud to write these twelve volumes that bear his name.

IV.

THE most distinguished member of a family of journalists, it was to be expected on general principles that Dr. Hale would, at some time of his life, become an editor. He has not merely realized this reasonable expectation, but has had a longer and a more diversified editorial experience than falls to the lot of most men who choose this as their sole calling. He began his apprenticeship to journalism as a mere boy, learning to set type in his father's printing-office. It is said of him, and one can easily believe it to be true, that at one time or another he has served in every capacity on the Boston "Advertiser," from reporter up to editor-in-chief. The magazines and weekly newspapers that he has edited would make a respectable catalogue by themselves, and include the "Christian Examiner," "Old and New," "Lend a Hand," and "The New England Magazine." Several periodicals which he has been chiefly instrumental in founding, and edited for a time, either maintain a prosperous existence still or have been absorbed into other ventures still more successful.

Dr. Hale has always made an admirable editor. He is industrious, methodical, enterprising; he writes well himself, and he is a good judge of others' work; he knows what the people will read, and at the same time has a high ideal of what they ought to read; and he has the faculty of gathering about him a corps of contributors, and inspiring them with his own enthusiastic purposes. Had he chosen to devote himself fully to daily journalism, what an editor he would have been! He would have preserved all the best traditions of the Greeley and Raymond school, adding to them a scholarship and a culture that the men of that school too often lacked, and bringing to his work a tone of high-mindedness and Christian principle, without the cant of religion, that daily journalism sorely needs.

V.

MANY would regard Dr. Hale's work as a philanthropist as the crown of a busy and diversified career, though it has been incidental, almost accidental, in his work as a man of letters. It is not an uncommon thing for the publication of a book to become the occasion of a doctrinal propaganda. Rousseau's "Le Contrat Social" is a classic instance, and in our own day Mr. Henry George's "Progress and Poverty," and Mr. Edward Bellamy's "Looking Backward" have furnished other illustrations. It is not by any means so common for a book to give rise to a practical philanthropic movement based on the highest Christian morality. Dr. Hale's "Ten Times One is

Ten " (Boston, 1870), had this unusual good fortune, thus achieving a success that its author undoubtedly places far above any commercial success attained by his stories. The hero of this tale, Harry Wadsworth, had for his motto: "Look up and not down; look forward and not back; look out and not in; and lend a hand." These clubs of ten, whose formation and method of work were suggested by this book, have very generally been called "Harry Wadsworth clubs," but, under whatever name, they have extended pretty much around the globe, having representatives not merely on this continent and in Europe, where we might reasonably expect them, but in Asia and Africa and the islands of the Pacific. This was the first successful attempt to enlist young people in Christian work, and was the parent idea to which may be traced the later success of other organizations, like the King's Daughters; and the Young People's Society of Christian Endeavor. The idea of the "Ten" as the unit of organization in the King's Daughters was borrowed directly from Dr. Hale; while its distinctive motto was probably suggested by the publication of another of his stories, "In His Name" (Boston, 1874), a tale of the Waldenses. There seems to be but one reason why these clubs did not have the same rapid growth in membership that the later organizations have had, namely, a prejudice against them in "orthodox" circles, owing to the fact that the clubs originated among Unitarians, — a very unworthy feeling, no doubt, but one quite inevitable in the present division of Protestant Christianity into a multitude of warring sects. Even with this drawback, in a little more than five years after the beginning of the movement these clubs counted a membership of fifty thousand.

Dr. Hale was a pioneer also in another hopeful cause, the enlistment of young children in religious enterprises. The "Look-up Legion" that he was instrumental in organizing among the children of the Sunday-schools, has had its counterpart in "Band of Hope" temperance societies, in the "Junior Societies" of Christian Endeavor, and in the still more recent "Boys' Brigade." All of these organizations, though each proceeds on lines of its own, rest on the principle, to which Dr. Hale was among the first to give outward expression, that formation is better than reformation, — that we may far easier mould character aright during its plastic stage than remake it when it has hardened into an immoral and un-Christian shape.

One must not fail to record Dr. Hale's enthusiastic and intelligent championship of popular education. He was one of the earliest and has been one of the most constant friends of the Chautauquan idea. From his pen have come some of the most enticing text-books of the Chautauqua courses, — though one must, in good conscience, add that they have not always been equal, in accuracy of detail, to the spirit in which they

Chautauqua.

were conceived. He has been a favorite lecturer at the summer school that meets yearly in the Chautauqua assembly. Not only in connection with this movement, but throughout all his career, by voice and pen he has stood for the American idea of popular sovereignty, but the sovereignty of a people trained in the fear of God and in the knowledge of God's world.

It is probable, nay, morally certain, that this account of Dr. Hale's protean activity fails to do him more than approximate justice. He has lived so full a life, that only an official biographer, with access to his papers and documents, can do more than vaguely outline the scope of his activities. The injunction of Scripture, "Whatsoever thy hand findeth to do, do it with thy might," he has fulfilled more completely than most men, and his hands have found so many things to do! Such a life reminds one of the Indian proverb, quoted by Sir William Jones, "Words are the daughters of earth, and deeds are the sons of heaven."

VI.

It may seem to some readers somewhat incongruous to assign so much space, in an essay ostensibly devoted to literary criticism, to the non-literary undertakings of a man like His power. Dr. Hale. Yet the procedure has its justification. To know any man's books it is a great help, if not

an indispensable requisite, to know the man. It
is also necessary, to judge the books properly, to
know what has been accomplished through them.
There are American authors who have written books
more perfect in form than those of Dr. Hale; but
his books, as the history of many of them has
proved, have a power such as few American authors
have shown. A marble statue may be more perfect, in the artist's judgment, than a living man;
but the living man, capable of conceiving and
achieving great things, is worth more to the world
than the lifeless marble with all its perfections.
Dr. Hale's books may not live in the literature of
the future, — that is, some of them may not, — but
they will survive through all generations in the
characters of men and women made nobler and
stronger through their influence.

A still further apology may be made for any
shortcomings in this account of the purely literary
work of Dr. Hale. It is so appallingly voluminous
Voluminous- in extent. He has written and published
ness.   fifty volumes; a complete bibliography
would make the number rather over than under the
half-hundred mark. It would be manifestly absurd,
with such a row of books staring him in the face,
for a critic to attempt anything like a detailed
examination of them in less space than an entire
volume. The most that can be done is to select
representatives of each class, and thus give a fairly
comprehensive account of the work as a whole,

without attempting exhaustive completeness. This is what has been attempted in this paper, and only a few things remain to be said by way of summing up.

Dr. Hale, in nearly all that he has written, has had a higher purpose than merely to amuse; in spirit and aim he has always been the _{Always the} preacher, whatever he may have been _{preacher,} doing. To say this will be to pronounce his condemnation, in the judgment of some narrow theorists, who prate of "art for art's sake," as if all truth had been finally committed to their hands for exposition and defence. But if Dr. Hale has always been preacher, as man of letters he has always been artist. His professional fondness for homiletics has never confused in his mind the distinction between sermon and story. Hence, while his fiction always preaches, it is never "preachy." He has learned the secret of teaching without didacticism. He never wrote a novel without purpose, and he never wrote a novel with a pur- _{but not} pose. This is paradox: it is also truth. _{"preachy."} He so tells a story that it makes its own impression, and a word of formal preaching would mar the effect. The fictitious history of "The Man Without a Country" is an excellent example of his achievement in this line. It was published during the throes of our civil war, at a time when its author wished to make the strongest plea in his power for loyalty to our country and its flag. It made a

profound impression, and it is hardly an exaggeration to say that the story of Philip Nolan was
worth as much to the Union cause, in its effect on
the *morale* of the people at a critical time, as a
victory won by our armies. Only those who put
bullet above brain, and mortars before morals, will
belittle the effect of such a story. Great as it is,
judged purely by literary standards as a piece of
composition, it is greater as a sermon.

One thing is remarkable in all of Dr. Hale's
writing, and that is his cheerful optimism. One
can recall nothing in his books at variance with
this dominant "note." He does not, indeed, go to
the extreme of maintaining that this is the best of
all possible worlds, and that whatever is is right;
but his heart ever sings with Pippa,—

> " God 's in his heaven —
> All 's right with the world ! "

He believes, in every drop of his blood, in the
fatherhood of God and the brotherhood of man. It is
a short creed, but there is none better; and on the
practical side of it, we are assured on excellent
authority, hang all the law and the prophets.
Thus believing, Dr. Hale holds that the
amelioration of the race is hopeful, and
the strength of this hope is in the possibility
of leading men to recognize their divine sonship.
It is a levelling up, therefore, not a levelling down,
toward which he directs his energies and his hopes.

His optimism.

"You are my brother," says Tolstoi, to the poor and degraded, "and therefore I will live with you and be dirty." "You are my brother," says Dr. Hale, "therefore live with me and be clean." This brief apologue illustrates two very different modes of approaching current problems relating to mankind and its social advancement. Much — not all, but much — of that which passes under the name of socialism belongs to the first category. Who of us will hesitate to proclaim his belief that Dr. Hale has found the more excellent way?

One takes leave of the Boston preacher, author, and philanthropist with regret. His is a nature cast in a large mould, a mind broad and hospitable to all truth, a soul instinct with faith, hope, and charity. Such a man, write he never so much, will necessarily be greater than any or all of his works. He cannot be measured by the standards of mathematics, for in him the whole is indefinitely greater than the sum of all its parts.

XV.

EDWARD EGGLESTON.

A VERY interesting essay might be written on the advantages of ill-health to men of letters. Whether by accident or in obedience to some law of human nature, it has happened in the history of literature that some of the greatest achievements have been due to men of infirm body. Ancient literature produced no more industrious and eminent man of letters than Cicero, yet nearly all his life he struggled with ill-health. Calvin wrote a whole library of books, and he, too, lived in a chronic state of invalidism. Pascal, though the volume of his work is comparatively small, made some of the choicest contributions to French literature, and his life was one long disease. In American literature, we may cap these instances with the names of Francis Parkman and Edward Eggleston. What Mr. Parkman achieved, in spite of afflictions and discouragements that would have crippled a man of ordinary industry and firmness of will, is a tale that has been often told without losing any of its romance. The story of Dr. Eggleston's life is hardly less striking; and though no single achievement of his can be said to surpass, or perhaps to

The triumph of mind.

equal Mr. Parkman's work, in the sum it is proof of unsurpassed industry, dogged perseverance, and unflagging purpose.

I.

EDWARD EGGLESTON was born at Vevay, Ind., December 10, 1837. His father was a lawyer by profession and a Virginian by birth. He died, however, when his son was a lad of nine. From the day of his birth young Eggleston enjoyed poor health, as they say in New England. He was a delicate boy, whose very continuance in life seemed at times most uncertain; and because of this *His youth.* delicacy he was not only unable to join in the hearty out-door sports of other boys, but was prohibited from pursuing any systematic course of education. He spent hardly more months in school than Abraham Lincoln, and, like the more famous Hoosier boy, was almost entirely self-educated. In 1856 his health was so delicate that his life was despaired of, and he spent four months in Minnesota in an attempt to restore it. Returning somewhat stronger, he became a Methodist circuit rider.

The circuit rider of those days was an institution peculiar to the time and the country. There have been circuit riders elsewhere, but none of *A circuit rider.* the precise type that the far West produced in its pioneer days. These men of faith, carrying their library as well as their wardrobe in their saddle-bags, preached the gospel through the entire frontier region of America. Their houses of worship were God's own temples, the woods. They lived in the plainest manner, sharing all the hardships of the pioneer people, making hazardous journeys, in frequent danger from floods, from wild beasts, and from men even more savage. The circuit preacher had a parish that, as one of them said, " took in one half of creation, for it had no boundary on the West." In many cases he was hardly more literate than his hearers, and these were fortunate, indeed, if they could read their Bibles and write their names; yet these uncouth preachers led multitudes of men to Christ, built churches, and laid denominational foundations deep and broad throughout all the great West. The present generation has entered into their labors with far too little comprehension of the tribulation and self-denials that those labors entailed.

Mr. Eggleston was, undoubtedly, a better educated man than many of the circuit preachers, as well as a man of greater native force of mind. He would never have been an ordinary or even an uncultivated man, His self-culture. wherever his lot might have been cast. With a hunger for knowledge, he was certain to gratify this craving in some manner under any circumstances. Those who have read his writings know how much of an education in human nature this experience was to him, and what a great part it had in making the broad-minded, tolerant man that he became. The severity of these labors, in spite of the healthfulness of the out-of-door life, compelled him from time to time to desist and finally to abandon his calling altogether.

Just when Mr. Eggleston began to have leanings toward literary work it is not possible, with the light we now have, to say. What is certain is, that the outward beginnings of his literary career Journalist. may be found in his removal in 1866 to Evanston, Ill., and his acceptance of a position on the editorial staff of the " Little Corporal," one of the first and most popular of American periodicals for the young. During his connection with it the quality of this paper was very much bettered, and up to the time of its sale to the newly established " St. Nicholas " it was, on the whole, the best periodical of its class. This journalistic experience in the West was extended by several years' service on the staff of the " Sunday-school Teacher " in Chicago, during which time the circulation leaped from five thousand to thirty-five thousand copies, — an emphatic testimony to the faithfulness and ability of his work.

In 1870 Dr. Eggleston came to New York. He was at first the literary editor of the " Independent," and for a time succeeded Theodore Tilton as editor of that newspaper. In 1871 he was editor of " Hearth and Home," and with his resignation of this Comes to post two years later his editorial labors New York. ceased. He showed in all the positions that he filled that he had the true journalistic gift, and, had his health permitted the severe and unintermitting application that the calling requires, he would, without

question, have been one of the most brilliant of
American journalists.

From 1874 to 1879 Dr. Eggleston was pastor of
the Church of Christian Endeavor, Brooklyn. This
church was as independent in its ecclesiastical relations
as Dr. Eggleston himself has always been

Pastor.

in his thinking and ways of work. Never,
perhaps, a popular preacher in the accepted sense of
that term, he was one to whom multitudes of men and
women belonging to the unchurched classes naturally
gravitated. He had a message for many uneasy and
hungry souls that find it difficult to be satisfied with
the rigid creeds and the orthodox sermonizing of the
ordinary evangelical churches. That this class is at
present a large one in our great cities no one who is
familiar with the facts will question, and Dr. Eggleston,
during these five years, was received by many people
of this type as a prophet of God. They were instructed, and, best of all, they were stimulated to holy
living and good works by his preaching. His church
was known as eminently a working church, a practical
church. Some of his methods for reaching and hold-
ing young men scandalized the staid orthodox people
of Brooklyn; but if they did not accomplish all the
good that he expected, it does not appear that they
ever did any serious harm.

Since his retirement from this pastorate, Dr. Eggleston has devoted himself entirely to literary work.
His residence for half the year is still in Brooklyn,
but during the other half-year he lives at Owls' Nest,

a picturesque cottage, beautifully situated on the shore of Lake George. Here he keeps his library, — a collection of some four thousand volumes, the greater part relating to colonial history, — and here he does his writing.

II.

DR. EGGLESTON'S first venture in pure literature, as distinguished from ephemeral journalistic writing, was "The Hoosier Schoolmaster." This story was published as a serial in "Hearth and Home" during the opening year of his editorship of that periodical, and was written in the midst of absorbing labors of all sorts, such as fall to the lot of every editor. The publication as a serial was begun before the story was more than well planned, and throughout its continuance the author was compelled to labor almost literally with the "devil" at his elbow. The novel made a sensation from the outset; indeed, how could it be otherwise? Not only had it great merits as a story, but it was so evidently written out of the author's heart and experience that no reader could fail to be impressed by its truth to life. It was a tale of great freshness, too. The pioneer preacher had become a pioneer in fiction. At that time (1871) few American writers had begun to suspect what a wealth of material existed for the novelist in our own country, especially in the West and South. The seaboard States had been exploited to some extent,

First story.

though the material was by no means exhausted, and the fame of Bret Harte was already abroad in the land; but in dealing with pioneer life in the newer West Dr. Eggleston was breaking soil as virgin as that of its own prairies.

There followed in due time several other books of the same general character, even better in literary finish and of similar flavor: "The Circuit Rider" (1874), "Roxy" (1878), "The Hoosier Schoolboy" (1883), and "The Graysons" (1887). "Roxy" and "The Graysons" were first published as serials in Other books. "The Century," and made the author known to a wider circle of readers than he had before possessed, and also gave to his writings the stamp of critical approval so highly valued by some. Before this time certain critics and readers had affected to look on Eggleston as an undisciplined product of the Wild West, hardly to be ranked alongside of the more cultured writers of the East. When he was taken up by one of the foremost periodicals of the world, it was necessary to revise this provincial judgment and award him his due place among our chief writers of fiction.

Of late years Dr. Eggleston has written less fiction, and in what he has written he has confined himself less closely to Hoosierdom. He has lived long enough now in the East to know it as well as he knows the West, better perhaps than he knows the Later writings. West of to-day, and he probably judged wisely in giving more of scope and variety to his work.

"The Faith Doctor," with its study of Christian Science and faith cure, was remarkable not only for its up-to-date, *fin de siècle* treatment of current speculation and social phenomena, but for its very accurate local color. It was quite distinctly the novel of the season when published. Rumor has it that Dr. Eggleston will write no more fiction, but will devote his remaining days to his labors as a historian.

It would be easy to analyze Dr. Eggleston's fictions, and to show in detail their literary excellence, but the task is in his case as superfluous as it might be tedious, for his chief excellence is not literary. He is, to be sure, a conscientious and artistic The man greater than the artist. writer, and in the technicalities of his craft he has nothing to fear from a comparison with others. What is meant in saying that his chief excellence is not literary is, that in him the artist is subordinate to the man. It does not require an intimate acquaintance with him to convince one that his is a personality that

" Shows a heart within blood-tinctured, of a veined humanity."

His closest friends describe him as a born philanthropist, whose house, wherever he may dwell, is thronged with those who stand in need of material or spiritual comfort, and who never depart unclothed and unfed. These ministrations are never professional and perfunctory, but are rendered in the spirit of Christian brotherhood. It is the throb of this warm and true heart, with its love for all humankind, its sympathy with human sorrows, its pity for human weakness, its tolerance of human errors, that one feels in Dr. Eggleston's books, and in this his peculiar charm and power must be sought.

III.

DR. EGGLESTON'S determination to give us no more novels, in spite of the high rank he has won as a writer of fiction, is understood to be due to his absorption in historical study. This is in no sense a sudden change of purpose, a transference of interest from one branch of the literary profession
Historian. to another, such as sometimes results from whim or ennui. One could comprehend how a popular novelist might become unspeakably weary of producing his novel a year, and how in sheer desperation and poverty of soul he might turn to other work for relief. So far as appears, Dr. Eggleston does not cease to write fiction because he is tired of it, and certainly he does not cease because the public is tired of him. He has a conviction, however, that he can do work of higher quality, of more lasting value, as a writer of history. Probably this conviction is well founded, and at any rate he is quite right to refuse to do what his conscience tells him is not the best of which he is capable, whether for the present the world agrees with him or no. It is more than likely that the world will disagree with him, for it loves to be amused and hates to be instructed.

The study of history, and the writing of it too, is, as has been intimated, not a recent pursuit of Dr. Eggleston's. It has more or less employed him throughout his busy career, and in these latter years may fairly be called the passion of his life. Long years ago he began to collect books relating to the colonial period of American history. This labor of love he has continued until he is said to have a collection of volumes, old and new, of every conceivable date, style, and condition, such as it would be hard to duplicate outside of our great Diligence in public libraries, if it could be duplicated research. even there. The libraries and book-stalls of Europe, as well as those of America, have been ransacked for the making of this collection. Besides, he has accumulated a mass of old prints, casts, manuscripts, autographs, curios, and relics of all sorts, that are something more than mere rarities to be gazed at, and are invaluable for illustrating his text. This reproducing to the eye the features of colonial life is something that has never before been attempted in a serious and systematic way, and its value cannot be overestimated. No one who is familiar with Knight's "Pictorial History of England," or with the illustrated edition of Green, will be disposed to undervalue the worth of a like service performed by a competent scholar, with rare industry and accuracy, for our own history.

Dr. Eggleston's first contributions to American history took the form of biographies of celebrated

17

Indians.   First came "Tecumseh" (1878), followed
speedily by "Pocahontas and Powhattan" (1879),
"Brant and Red Jacket" (same year), "Montezuma
and the Conquest of Mexico" (1880).   With the
exception of the last-named book, these
biographies still have the field pretty
much to themselves, and are likely to hold it for
some time to come.   Though these worthies figure
of necessity in every history of America, most historians content themselves with giving them a para-
graph, or at most a page, each.   Dr. Eggleston
found abundant materials for full-length biographies;
and the freshness of the subjects and the completeness of the research on which the books were
founded, recommended them to popular favor hardly
less than the animated style in which they were
written.

In 1888 was published a "History of the United
States," in two single-volume editions, one for school
use, the other for general reading, and so appropri-
ately called a "Household edition."   It was by no
means a waste of his time or talents for an author
like Dr. Eggleston to undertake such a work, for to
produce a really good popular history is
an end worthy of any man's ambition.
This history is ideally good, thanks to the writer's
skill and the publishers' liberality.   The house of
Appletons is justly famous for its illustrated books;
but though it has issued volumes far more costly and
of greater significance as works of art, its imprint has

never been placed on a book in which art has been
more successfully made the handmaid of history.
The illustrations were selected and have been executed with the purpose of combining artistic excellence with historic significance, and this mark has
been hit with great accuracy. The text is almost
as pictorial as the illustrations; the author has caught
the secret of presenting our country's history in a
manner that may fairly be described as panoramic.
Though intended for young readers especially, it
has been quite as fully appreciated by their elders,
who value it as the best brief history of their country
that has yet been published.

The *chef d'œuvre* of Dr. Eggleston, the culmination of life-long study and many years' exclusive toil,
is a history of the American people. The title has
been announced in various forms, such as " History of
Life in the United States," and "Life in the His *chef*
Thirteen Colonies," — or, perhaps, the latter *d'œuvre.*
is only a sub-section of a larger work. Chapters of
this work have already appeared in "The Century,"
and have aroused expectation to a very high pitch.
Compared with the form in which it will ultimately
appear, this serial publication may be regarded as,
in a sense, only the first rough draft; and this being
the case, we are warranted in expecting that the
completed form will be one of the most important
historic books of our century.

That this is no exaggerated estimate will appear
from a critical examination of what has already been

printed. There are histories of the United States in
great plenty, and many of them have extraordinary
Life of the people. merit. There is no history, however, that
adequately records the facts of, and traces
the development in, the life of the people. It would
be uncritical to depreciate the value of those histories
that devote themselves chiefly to a record of events;
that follow the rise, growth, and decay of political
parties, or thread the mazes of diplomacy; that describe great campaigns and the single battles which
have decided the destiny of the continent; that trace
the marvellous development of industry and commerce. All of these things are important, instructive, and interesting, but they are not the history of
the people. We still wish to know what manner of
men and women our forefathers were, how and what
they ate and drank and wherewithal they were clothed,
what houses they lived in, and what other creature
comforts they enjoyed. We wish to understand their
social customs, to penetrate the secret of their religious life, even to hear their daily gossip. It is not
beneath the dignity of history to concern itself about
such things, and we cannot say that we have mastered
any period until we have gained such knowledge of it.

That Dr. Eggleston is capable of doing this sort of
work incomparably well he has already given proof.
He has now spent a decade, in almost entire exclu-
sion of other labors, on this work; and when the
stately volumes appear, they cannot fail fitly to crown
a long, a varied, a useful, a highly honorable life.

XVI.

GEORGE WASHINGTON CABLE.

ONE hesitates whether to call Mr. Cable a representative Southern writer, for such a characterization might give offence. And yet, considering the writings by which he is chiefly known and on which his fame must hereafter rest, one does not know what other description would suit the case. If a man born and bred in the South, of an old Southern family, whose fictions are saturated with the South and reflect its life with photographic accuracy, — if such a man may not be said to be a representative Southern writer, to whom How far a Southern may that phrase be applied? It is true writer. that of late years Mr. Cable has become out of favor in the South, that his name is rarely spoken there without some adjective of condemnation or execration, but this state of things has no connection with literature proper. It is not because of his novels, but because of certain political writings of his, that Mr. Cable has thus lost the favor of those among whom he was born and bred, for whom he shed his blood, and with whom he has spent the greater part of his life. The son and grandson of slaveholders,

he has dared to plead the cause of the ex-slave, dared
to oppose the dominant idea of his native State,
dared to speak the truth as he sees it, though in a
minority of one.   This is his sin, and the South has
pronounced it to be unpardonable.   Leaving for the
present this political question wholly to one side,
let us consider the purely literary part of Mr.
Cable's work.   Most of this was produced before
his political heresies were promulgated, and has
been neither bettered nor spoiled by those heresies.
It has, therefore, a double claim on our impartial
consideration.   Even those who condemn most
strongly the treason of Benedict Arnold do not
withhold their praise of his services at Quebec,
Lake Champlain, and Saratoga.   In like manner
even they who regard Mr. Cable as a traitor to his
race, his State, and his party, may without incon-
sistency, and should in justice, consider his earlier
writings apart from his later.

I.

MR. CABLE was born in New Orleans, October
12, 1844.   Through his father he is descended from
a Virginia family of German origin.   His mother
was a New Englander, and from her the novelist
derives that strain of Puritanism so evident in his
character as in his work.

It is good for a man to bear the yoke in his
youth, to have his sinews toughened and his will

braced by a struggle with poverty, provided he really is a man and not a weakling. The elder Cable was a prosperous man of business until 1849, when he failed. After his ^{A toilsome youth.} death in 1859, at an age when most boys have noth-ing to think of but books and play, young Cable was compelled to share the support of the family. He never grumbled, though he was a studious lad who would have liked and profited by a liberal education. He had a liberal education indeed,— not in any col-lege, but in the school of adversity,— and it made of him a man thoroughly trained, completely equipped, able to hold his own with any.

Hardly had young Cable begun a mercantile career as clerk in a New Orleans house when the Civil War broke out. He was too young to serve in the army at first, though his ^{Confederate soldier.} sympathies were naturally with his State and the South; but in 1863 he enlisted in the Fourth Mississippi Cavalry, and remained in the service till the close of the war. He was a good soldier, and bears some honorable scars to testify to his valor. After the war he had a somewhat checkered life, — now a clerk, afterwards a member of a sur-veying and exploring party; in which latter work he contracted a severe malarial fever, from which he was two years in recovering. This was by no means lost time, however, for in these years he accumulated much of the material of which later he made so good use.

II.

MR. CABLE, like many other American writers, made his first literary venture in journalism. He *Journalism.* began as an occasional contributor to the "New Orleans Picayune," and as his communications found favor he increased their frequency until he came to be regarded as a member of the staff. The story has been told that his connection with the paper was abruptly severed by his refusal, on conscientious grounds, to write a theatrical criticism that had been assigned him, but his own version is much more prosaic: "The true cause of my dismissal was simply that as a reporter I was a failure." After this he sought and obtained employment as clerk in a cotton-broker's office, and found a more profitable market for his writings at the North. It was about this time that "Scribner's Monthly" began to publish short tales of Creole life by Mr. Cable. From the first these received a warm welcome, which was due solely to their merits, for the writer was unheralded and unknown. They were something entirely new in literature. *First stories.* Nobody, with knowledge of the theme and ability to treat it, had seriously attempted to depict the Creole in fiction, and Mr. Cable was therefore fortunate enough to offer the novel-reader that which he dearly loves, an entirely new sensation. The true epicure does not welcome with more enthusiasm a cook who has invented a new and delicious sauce, than the devotee of the novel shows in the reception of a writer who transports him into the midst of hitherto unknown types of character and a strange social atmosphere.

These stories were written under difficulties that would have discouraged most men. The author's clerical employment filled the ordinary working hours of the day, and he was compelled to do his work in minutes snatched from what time most young men give to sleep or social relaxation. It was his habit to rise at four o'clock and write before breakfast, and some of his best work was done in these early morning hours. Those who maintain that if a young man has any genius in him it will somehow find expression under the most unfavorable circumstances, will find much to support their thesis in the life of Mr. Cable. After all, we probably waste our sentiment on the "mute, inglorious Miltons" and those "who die with all their music in them" of whom poets sing so pathetically. Mute, inglorious Miltons and voiceless singers they would doubtless have remained had they Per aspera been born with golden spoons in their ad astra. mouths. But such application as Mr. Cable's is trying to nerve and muscle, and we need not wonder that this constant brain and pen work caused more than one break-down in health. It was fortunate for him that the death of the head of his house in 1879 again left him without employment, and in a way forced him to take the bold step of devoting himself to literature. It was a great risk; for though he had won a place for himself as a magazine writer, he had yet to show that he had staying power or was capable of something really great. Only one of a thousand succeeds in such an experiment, but Mr. Cable proceeded to prove that he was one of a thousand.

III.

THE same year that marked the beginning of a purely literary life saw the publication of Mr.

Creole life in fiction.
Cable's first volume, "Old Creole Days," a collection of seven stories of Creole life. They had not only the good fortune already mentioned, of freshness of substance, but the additional advantage of novelty of form. Mr. Cable was one of the pioneers in the dialect tale, and dialect was not reckoned in those days as something to be forgiven an author, but as one of his titles to distinction, provided it were skilfully managed. The "New Orleans Picayune" was at that time proud of the fledgling it had shoved out from the nest to try his wings in literature, and not afraid to speak the truth about him; so it said: "The careful rendering of the Creole dialect reveals patient study of living models; and to any reader whose ear is accustomed to the broken English as heard in the parts of our city every day, its truth to nature is

striking." It hardly needed testimony of this kind
to establish the accuracy of Mr. Cable's literary
methods, for his stories are self-evidencing, and
anybody who should challenge their faithfulness
would have a large fund of incredulity to overcome.
The adequacy of his representations of Creole life
has, indeed, been challenged by authorities worthy
of respect. It is one thing to maintain that his
work is faithful as far as it goes, and another to
hold that it is exhaustive. Mr. Cable has never
made this absurd claim, and no friend has made it
on his behalf.

These stories established their author's right to
be numbered with the greatest artists of American
literature. It has appeared from his history that he is mainly a self-educated   Great artist.
man, with no literary atmosphere, no association
with men of letters, to influence his development.
So far as can be judged, until he was able to buy
for himself, his access to books was very limited.
A natural aptitude for literature, an innate gift of
expression, improved by much practice and severe
self-criticism, gave him command of a style almost
perfect for his purposes. It is a style of limpid
clearness, of easy grace, not much given to orna-
mentation, and pleasingly destitute of mannerisms;
a style of pure English, instinct with life and
passion, sometimes reaching the borderland of
poetry, but still oftener delighting by its delicate
humor. In these stories laughter and tears lie near

together, their pathos and even tragedy being as
true and moving as their humor.   It is seldom
given to any author to sweep the whole gamut of
human emotions with a touch so sure, yet so light
and easeful, as that of Mr. Cable.

This first volume, delightful as it was, did not
prove that the author had the constructive power

Novels.   necessary to the writing of a novel.   He
              might easily have been such an one as
Bret Harte, a writer of unsurpassed short stories
who loses his cunning when he undertakes to fill in
a large canvas.   A painter would say of a writer of
this type that his drawing and coloring are good,
but that he cannot compose.   Mr. Cable set all
doubts of his quality at rest by immediately producing "The Grandissimes," which, after running
as a serial in "Scribner's," was published in book
form in 1880.   This was followed in 1881 by
"Madame Delphine," and in 1883 by "Dr. Sevier."
Here is a trio of books not easily equalled in recent American literature, and probably never surpassed, certainly not among fictions distinctively
"American."   For not the most fastidious of foreign critics can withhold that adjective from Mr.
Cable's work, it is so obviously autochthonous, —
it could by no possibility have been written by
any one but an American who had studied the
Creole character from the life, and had known from
boyhood the scenes among which his characters
move.

Since the publication of these books Mr. Cable has produced no more novels, though he has written a number of stories that might be called novelettes. Three of these — "Grande Pointe," "Carancro," and "Au Large" — have been included in one volume under the general title of "Bonaventure" (1887). This book, one is justified in saying, is not so much a novel as a collection of novelettes. A still more recent book, "Strange True Stories of Louisiana," is rather compiled and revised by Mr. Cable than written by him, being composed of manuscripts by various inexperienced writers, that he has retouched. This is a sort of literary collaboration that is likely to cause him more annoyance than it can bring him fame, since some of the original writers have made public accusations of unfair treatment, which, however unfounded they are, must be unpleasant in the extreme.

It would not be fair to say that in the trio of novels above named Mr. Cable had exhausted his resources, but we are perhaps warranted in concluding that in them his genius found, for the time at least, its full expression, since in the ten years that succeeded the publication of "Dr. Sevier" he had no other message of the kind to speak to the world. By waiting until "the angel says, Write," he proved that he respects himself, his public, and his art too much to produce his yearly volume, whether it be good or bad.

Later writings.

IV.

MR. CABLE is remarkable among American novelists for a rare combination of æsthetic and religious
endowments. In no other American fiction, unless it be in Hawthorne's, do we find the highest artistic instinct and the profoundest moral purpose so wedded. In truth, even the exception of Hawthorne cannot be allowed, for he is psychologic rather than moral, an observer and analyzer of moral problems, and coldly critical, not sympathetic, in his treatment of them. But in Mr. Cable the moral purpose is almost stronger than the æsthetic instinct; rather they exist in his work in a balance so perfect that neither can be said to overtop the other. The worship of the beautiful and the worship of the good are in general unequally yoked together when they are united at all. We have æsthetes in plenty, like Wilde and Pater, who will discourse eloquently on the holiness of beauty; and there is no lack of divines who will discourse with equal eloquence on the beauty of holiness; but not to one man of letters in generations is it given to see and to understand and to embody both.

A rare combination.

It is this unique combination that has embroiled Mr. Cable with his former friends and admirers in the South. All that he afterwards said in "The Silent South" and "The Negro Question" is potentially present in his fiction. He

Slavery.

is, as has been said before, the son of one slave-
holder and the grandson of another,— of two others,
for that matter, — but nothing can make one believe
that he could ever have been a slave-owner himself,
not even if slaves had come to him by inheritance.
If this seems too positive an utterance, let the
doubter read the history of Bras-Coupé in "The
Grandissimes." No abolitionist ever scourged the
institution of slavery with words more fiery than
those that tell that hideous tale. Yet Southerners
tolerated this, if they did not precisely admire it.
The reason is plain: slavery was a defunct institution, and nothing in this world is deader than a
dead political issue. Slavery, that caused the blood-
iest civil war known to history in 1861, had not a
living apologist twenty years later; and where a
disrespectful word would once have been another
name for suicide, burning sarcasm and piercing
irony passed unresented if not quite approved.

But when Mr. Cable ventured to touch a political
question of his day, when he tired of denouncing a
dead abuse and dared to drag into the Unpopularity
light a monstrous living wrong, — ah, that in the South.
was quite another story. Languid indifference
changed with the rapidity of thought to fierce
hatred. Toleration gave place to abuse, and would
have given place to persecution had not Mr. Cable,
fortunately for himself, placed himself beyond the
reach of anything but bad language. This outburst
of impotent rage was far from creditable to the

South.   Mr. Cable may have been wrong, — many Northern readers, who might be expected to agree with him, think that he is wrong, or at any rate only partially right, — but his courage was worthy of respect, and he should have been answered with fact and argument, not with billingsgate.   Even less creditable than their angry replies has been the suggestion by Southern writers of unworthy motives on Mr. Cable's part, — that he desired to curry favor with his Northern public, and to do this was willing to turn his pen against his own people.   The insinuation is worse than base, it is silly.   Mr. Cable

Courage that deserved admiration.   already had the favor of Northern readers, and he had nothing further to desire in this direction.   He was recognized as the peer of Howells and James and Aldrich, and whatever he might write on political or social questions could not set him higher.   Without the possibility or the hope of advancing his own fortunes, he deliberately risked his popularity among his own people to tell them what he believed to be the truth.   Courage like this deserved the admiration that we of the North do not hesitate to award to the valor of those who fought so well in what we firmly believe to have been a bad cause.

Perhaps the feeling against Mr. Cable in the South is due not merely to what he has written,

Residence in the North.   but to the fact that he has taken up his residence in the North.   It should be borne in mind, however, that the temptation for a

Southern man of letters to do this is almost over-whelming. However proud the South may be of its writers, it does not offer them an adequate sup-port. It is Northern capital that publishes the books of Southern writers. Northern enterprise pushes their sale, and Northern readers for the most part buy them. A writer who chooses, as Mr. Cable did for several years, to add to his income by giving public readings from his writings, must look to Northern cities for his audiences. Since this is so, and so long as it continues to be so, a Northern residence must offer great advan-tages. It is a convenience for a writer to be near his publishers, for a lecturer to be within easy reach of his audiences, even in these days when telegraph and fast express almost annihilate space. Besides, since when has a man lost the right in free America to live where he chooses and to change his resi-dence as often as he pleases?

The feeling against Mr. Cable will pass away. His political writings are a mere episode in his life, and are necessarily ephemeral. In after years the antiquarian and the historian may curiously peer into their pages, if perchance a copy survives, but his fictions are as imperishable as the language. The South will yet come to a better mind, and will see in Mr. Cable one of her most gifted sons, — not infallible, but honest, high-minded, and courageous, possessed, **in a word**, of the very virtues always

18

most admired and cherished by his compatriots. And his books will stand forth, while American literature is read, as a perfect picture of a unique civilization, unsurpassed in finish among the work of his time, and inspired by that love of God and one's neighbor which is more than all whole burnt offerings and sacrifices.

XVII.

RICHARD HENRY STODDARD.

"LITERATURE is a great staff, but a sorry
crutch." That is as true to-day as when
Scott said it, and it is true, because, in the words of
Mr. Froude, "literature happens to be the only occupation in which wages are not given in proportion
to the goodness of the work done." It is doubtless a
fact that the born writer finds in his labor his highest
compensation, but this is no more true of "The times
are out of
him than of any other worker who puts joint."
heart and soul into his occupation, and is not a mere
hireling. The laborer is worthy of his hire, whatever
his labor. Whoever devotes himself to an occupation
that has for its result the ennobling of his race, the
enrichment of men's minds, the enlargement of their
field of mental and moral vision, is fairly entitled to a
comfortable living. The world owes at least this to
him. And yet, unless he possesses the happy faculty
of making his writings salable, unless he is willing to
produce merely what men will buy and leave undone
the higher work of which he is capable, the writer
may starve for all the world cares. The life and
work of Mr. Stoddard are a saddening instance

of the short-sightedness of mankind, of the imperfection of our present social order, of the way in which a man may be compelled to waste endowments of a high order, that he may wring from a niggard world a bare subsistence.

I.

MR. STODDARD was born in Hingham, Mass., July 2, 1825. He lost his father, a sea-captain, at an early age, and in 1835 his mother, who had married again, **Early years.** removed to New York. Since then his life has been identified with the life of the metropolis. His education, such as it was, he gained in the public schools of the city, but it could not have extended beyond a rather limited course in the ordinary English branches. While still a mere lad he went to work in an iron foundry, and remained there several years. Had he been just an ordinary, average boy, with a shrewd gift of making a good bargain and a half-miserly capacity for saving money, and had he devoted himself with all his soul to the iron business, he might have died many times a millionnaire, envied by all and possibly respected by some. He chose the better part. He preferred lifelong poverty, comparatively speaking, and the culture of mind and heart, to wealth and narrowness. If, as Seneca thinks, the gods are well pleased when they see great men contending with adversity, Mr. Stoddard must have afforded the gods much delight, for his life has been one struggle with adverse fortune.

None of our American authors has begun a literary career with less of outward encouragement or with a more slender stock of endowment. By endowment, óne of course means visible qualification. For one so slightly educated, compelled to labor for daily bread, with neither leisure for culture nor friends to encourage and assist him, — for such a lad to cherish literary aspirations would have seemed to most people a ridiculous height of presumption. And so it would have been in one less clearly conscious of his calling. " Blessed are they that hunger and thirst after knowledge, for they shall be filled," is a beatitude not written in Scripture, it is true; but it is written in the divine order of the universe, and it was fulfilled in the case of young Stoddard. His evenings were given to the study of the best English authors, and particularly of the poets. Already his soul was fired with the thought that he too would yet be a poet.

Slight encouragement.

What did more than all else to develop this hope, this aspiration, into a reality was his good fortune in making the acquaintance of other young men of letters in New York, — Bayard Taylor, Edmund Clarence Stedman, Thomas Bailey Aldrich, and others. The acquaintance with Taylor was earliest, most intimate, and had the greatest effect on his character. Taylor was fresh from Europe and the publication of his " Views Afoot," which had given

Budding authors.

him a recognized standing among young authors.
Stoddard was his junior only a few months by the
calendar, but several years his junior in literary experience, and as yet wholly unknown to fame.   Both
had to give their days to hard toil, — Stoddard to his
foundry and Taylor to the "Tribune," where he
worked fifteen hours a day, scribbling leaders, book-
notices, foreign letters, and generally doing the work
now assigned to three or four men on the "Tribune"
staff.   Only their evenings were theirs, and of these
but one, Saturday evening, was really free.   These
Saturday nights were passed in each other's company,
and they were in a sense the making of Stoddard.
They drew out of him what was latent; intelligent and
sympathetic companionship supplemented the culture
he was gaining from books and the practice of composition, and under this genial stimulus his powers
rapidly expanded.

The same year (1849) that witnessed the beginning
of this friendship, which was to be broken only by
Footprints.   Taylor's untimely death, also saw the publication of the youthful poet's first volume
of verses, under the title of "Footprints."   It was
privately printed, and he was so little proud of it that
he afterward destroyed the edition.

> " 'T is pleasant, sure, to see one's name in print;
> A book 's a book, although there 's nothing in 't."

Many a young bardling enjoys this pleasure at his
own expense, but few have the grace to repent their
folly so promptly, and to repair it by the one means

in their power. There is hope for such, and their
second ventures are likely to be worthier of a better
fate.

Soon after this another great event befell the poet.
His friend Taylor went to Europe again. The young
poet was lonely, he had a present none too assured,
and a future still less certain, so he naturally married.
His fortune was better than perhaps so Marriage.
headlong an act deserved, and could
hardly have been greater had he acted with the most
approved worldly wisdom. Elizabeth Barstow, also
of Massachusetts birth, was the exact counterpart of
Mr. Stoddard in the other sex. She, too, was and is
a poet whose graceful verses are worthy of high praise,
but she has taken even higher rank as a novelist. It
is really one of the curiosities of literature that her
books have not won a wider recognition, a more
general admiration, from readers of American fiction.
They are high favorites, and have been from the first,
of those who are fitted to appreciate work of enduring
qualities, and they will continue to be read when current trash has fallen to its real value as junk. There
have been some signs of late that tardy fame is about
to overtake Mrs. Stoddard, and one hopes that the
event may justify this forecast. This union of hearts
and labors is almost the one instance of the kind in
American literature, — at least, it is almost the only
one that has endured for an ordinary lifetime all the
vicissitudes of fortune, growing more beautiful and
more helpful with every passing year.

II.

BY 1851 Mr. Stoddard was fairly launched in literature. He published that year a second volume of
verse, that ranked him at once among the promising
young poets; and this was followed in 1856 by " Songs
Songs of
Summer.　of Summer," which set his name still higher
on the roll. He found more fame than
dollars in poetry, however, and was compelled to turn
his hand to work of various kinds to secure a livelihood. Through Hawthorne's influence, it is said, he
obtained in 1853 a clerkship in the New York Custom
House, which he held until 1870, after which he held
other like positions for periods more or less brief,
until in 1879 he plunged into literature once for all,
sink or swim. He has never sunk, but one may
guess that he has often found it hard swimming.

It would not be easy to name the other American
author who has done so much hard work for so insig-
nificant pay. Mr. Stoddard has been all his life a
most laborious man, working harder than any mechanic
in town and receiving wages but little better than
those of a clever mechanic. Most of this labor has
Pegasus a
plough-horse.　been mere hack work. One says this in no
disparagement of Mr. Stoddard, or of the
usefulness of what he has done, but in hot indignation
of soul that Pegasus should thus be put to the plough.
It is we, the public, who are to blame for such a state
of things; we should take shame to ourselves that we

have allowed such a man to fritter away his powers
on work that any penny-a-liner could do, — not so
well, doubtless, but well enough. Mr. Stoddard has
not complained; he has borne his burden as a brave
man should, cheerfully, nobly, but the iron must have
entered into his soul.

The critic will be justified in passing by all of this
work with a brief word of praise for its conscientious-
ness. It was not written to live, but to live by. Mr.
Stoddard has written prose because he must; he
writes poetry because he cannot help it. His prose
writings may be, without any disrespect to them or
him, simply labelled "pot boilers" and laid aside.
They fulfilled their purpose when they His prose writings.
amused a passing hour, or set afloat again
a half-forgotten piece of standard literature. The
author deserves for this part of his labor precisely
the praise that a good maker of shoes deserves, —
he has put his heart and conscience into the task by
which he wins his daily bread, and has done it well.
But task work it is, and task work it will remain.

III.

THE case is totally different, however, when we
come to Mr. Stoddard's poetry. We are conscious
in a moment of breathing a different atmosphere.
In the prose writings we find him a workman, here
we find him an artist; in the former he is honest,

cultivated, painstaking, conscientious, but in the latter he is a man of genius.

Besides the volumes of verse already named, he published "The King's Bell" (1863), "The Book of the East" (1871), and a complete edition of his poetical works in 1880, which makes a book of nearly five hundred pages. This is not a remarkably bulky tome, considering the fact that it represents a lifetime's devotion to the muses; but when one also considers the dis-tractions and difficulties under which the work has been done, it is a striking proof of what has already been said, — that Mr. Stoddard writes poetry because he cannot help doing it.

Two books of verse.

The striking characteristic of the earlier poems, included in the edition of 1880, is the passionate love of beauty that inspires them. If one were to pay Mr. Stoddard the insulting compliment of call-ing him "The American ——," one would instinct-ively fill out the blank with the name of Keats after reading some of these poems. The style is not that of Keats, the resemblance is not verbal and formal, such as results from imita-tion; it is only that the youthful American poet was a twin soul of the Briton. If a reader should find such verses, for example, in a collection of extracts from Keats, he would feel no incongruity, though he might say, "From what poem by Keats are these taken? I do not remember to have seen them before."

Keats.

" From earliest infancy my heart was thine,
  With childish feet I trod thy temple aisles ;
  Not knowing tears, I worshipped thee with smiles,
Or if I wept it was with joy divine.
By day, and night, on land, and sea, and air,
    I saw thee everywhere.
A voice of greeting from the wind was sent,
  The mists enfolded me with soft white arms,
The birds did sing to lap me in content,
  The rivers wore their charms,
And every little daisy in the grass
Did look up in my face, and smile to see me pass."

These lines are taken from a "Hymn to the Beautiful;" and possibly the form of the stanza and its musical quality, as well as the title, might suggest to the reader Shelley and his "Hymn to Intellectual Beauty." But whatever poets may have strongly influenced Mr. Stoddard in his earlier years, no one poet dominated him. His was a catholic taste, a universal worship of the beautiful, and he could appreciate what was good or great in every English poet. As his mind matured, these suggestions of other poets disappear from his verse, and his style becomes more distinctive, more individual. The passion for beauty, however, does not become weaker. In the "Songs of Summer," published during the flower of his young manhood, there is almost a tropical luxuriance of feeling, and a prodigality of fancy not always matched by felicity of expression. The emphasis sometimes seems overstrained, and the thought is not always strictly

Prodigal fancy.

coherent.   Other American men of letters have
amused themselves by parodying this manner, sometimes with very amusing results.   There is, however, much verse in this collection that shows full
mastery of the poet's art, and some of the gems
that one can find here and there are of the first
water; for instance, this, —

> " The sky is a drinking-cup,
>   That was overturned of old,
> And it pours in the eyes of men
>   Its wine of airy gold.
>
> " We drink that wine all day,
>   Till the last drop is drained up,
> And we are lighted off to bed
>   By the jewels in the cup ! "

IV.

IN his later poems, Mr. Stoddard has essayed
some higher flights.   Some of his narrative poems
are rare examples of the art of telling a story in
verse; among which may be named " The King's
Bell," " The King's Sentinel," and " The Pearl of
the Philippines."   This is not a gift that is greatly
valued in these days, more's the pity, and the poet
who has it is pretty sure to conclude that

> " There's a luck in most things, and in none
> More than in being born at the right time ;
> It boots not what the labor to be done,
> Or feats of arms, or art, or building rhyme.
> Not that the heavens the little can make great,
> But many a man has lived an age too late."

Of a quality better appreciated by readers, if not more highly praised by critics, are such poems as the Horatian ode on Abraham Lincoln, Ode on Lincoln. which one is much inclined to pronounce not only the best thing Mr. Stoddard has ever written, but the best thing any poet has written on Lincoln, saving only Mr. Lowell's unapproached "Commemoration Ode." There are in it fewer lines felicitously quotable than in Lowell's ode, yet such as the following come little short of that excellence: —

> "One of the People! Born to be
>   Their curious epitome."

> "No hasty fool, of stubborn will,
>   But prudent, cautious, pliant still."

> . . . "his genius put to scorn
> The proudest in the purple born,
>   Whose wisdom never grew
>   To what, untaught, he knew."

Quite perfect, both in thought and expression, is the tender poem "Adsum," on the death of Thackeray; and quite as appreciative, though less tenderly pathetic, are the verses entitled "At Gadshill." One cannot highly commend what are perhaps the most ambitious performances in this edition of 1880, — "Guests of the State," a centen- Occasional poems. nial ode, and "History," a poem in Spenserian stanza read before the Phi Beta Kappa

Society of Harvard. To attempt to write a great poem for a great occasion is to invite failure, and the few who succeed do so by some fortunate accident. Occasional poems for the most part, except such witty and familiar verses as the "Autocrat" succeeded in turning off, have added more to the bulk than to the glory of American literature.

One who goes through this edition of Mr. Stoddard's verse carefully, checking off only those poems without which American literature would be distinctly poorer, will have a new idea of the extent and value of the work the poet has done. The contemporary fame of authors furnishes some of the most curious puzzles of literature. That Southey should ever have been considered a great poet while Shelley was practically unknown, is something that we of to-day can never fully comprehend; and the history of literature is full of just such strange facts. Mention the poems of Stoddard to intelligent and well-read friends, — who know their Lowell and Bryant, their Stedman and Aldrich, and who know Stoddard the clever magazinist and editor of books, — and one is likely to be met by the saying, "Why, I never knew that he wrote any poetry." So astounding ignorance in quarters where knowledge might fairly be expected is inexplicable, unless, indeed, it be due to this, that as prolific essayist and industrious editor, Mr. Stoddard has eclipsed himself as poet. Certainly, for whatever cause, he is less known to Americans,

Popular ignorance.

even to those who love the literature of their country, than he deserves to be. This cannot always remain true. The man who has a genuine call to write may say with Philip of Spain, "I and time against any two," — nay, against the world.

Much as he merits our praise and admiration for what he has actually done, this is a man who still more should receive our homage for what A priceless he has attempted. It is something in example. these days, when the sordid and selfish pursuit of wealth absorbs so much of what is best in the youth of America, to have this example of unswerving choice of the intellectual life. It is something, shall we say? It is a priceless thing, should rather be said. The average man of affairs, to whom getting rich is the chief end of man, and poverty the unpardonable sin, can see nothing but the extreme of folly in a life given to literature for the love of the work and not for love of its rewards. To those who know the true values of things there is an element of heroism, of greatness of soul, in such a life. America will never be quite given over to the worship of the Almighty Dollar, she will never be chained to Mammon's chariot wheels, while she has here and there a son who turns his face ever towards "the shining, unveiled face of truth."

XVIII.

FRANCIS RICHARD STOCKTON.

AMERICAN humor has now a world-wide repute, and is enjoyed if not appreciated by an
international audience. The goddess of fame has
been more lavish than discriminating in the distri-
bution of her favors to American humorists. It is
a single type of humor that has become known to
American foreign readers as distinctively American,
humor. — the type of which Artemus Ward and
Mark Twain (in a part of his writings) are the best
representatives. This humor is broad; it deals
largely in exaggeration; it produces gales of merriment by a fortunate jest; it lacks delicacy, constructive power, and literary form. Foreign critics,
who are more distinguished for refined taste than
for profound knowledge of things American, seldom
speak with much respect of American humor. It
may be well adapted, they concede, to tickle the
ears of the groundlings, but it makes the judicious
grieve. We who are to the manner born know the
weak spot in this criticism. We know that America
has produced another type of humor, and appreciate
at its true value the courtly polish of Irving, the

catholic and urbane manner of Lowell, the playful,
half-bantering earnestness of Warner. To this
school belongs the subject of this paper, and he
alone would redeem our humorists from the charge
of coarseness and want of literary charm.

I.

WHEN he first began writing fantastic tales for
children, the author signed them "Frank R. Stockton," and that name still holds its place
on the titlepages of his books. His
proper Christian names are, however, Francis
Richard, and he was born in Philadelphia, April
5, 1834. He had a good education, being graduated from the Central high-school of his native city
in 1852, but, like many of our successful American
authors, he did not have a college training. His
first choice of occupation was that of engraver and
draughtsman, but his bent was literary rather than
artistic, and he found his way into journalism. It
would have been rather remarkable had such not
been the case, as a marked tendency towards literature distinguishes his family. A younger brother
was a journalist of distinction; an elder half-
brother was an honored Methodist clergyman and
author; and a sister, though she has been somewhat
eclipsed by his greater fame, is known as a writer
of excellent stories for the magazines, and of several
books. Mr. Stockton was connected for **brief**

Early years.

periods with various newspapers and periodicals, and on the establishment of "St. Nicholas" became its assistant editor.   There is reason to believe that his editorial work was of excellent character; but both his tastes and his gifts were rather for original work, and for nearly or quite twenty years now he has given himself to the writing of stories.   As early as 1870 four of his tales for children were issued in book form by a Boston publisher, under the title of "The Ting-a ling Stories," and thereafter he was known to the initiated as "a promising writer."

Mr. Stockton first gained the ear of the great public in 1879, when a series of papers with a slight thread of story appeared serially in "Scribner's Monthly," and later in a volume, under the title of "Rudder Grange."   The story of the young couple keeping house in a canal-boat and taking a boarder was irresistibly funny, and the details were worked out with great skill. Euphemia and Pomona became household words at once; their droll sayings and droller doings gave many a pleasant hour of reminiscence, long after the enjoyment of the first reading had been experienced.   The supreme test of the quality of humor is its capacity to yield continuous pleasure.   There are things that make one laugh consumedly at first hearing, as if their author

Rudder Grange.

> " Had meant to put his whole wit in a jest,
>   And resolved to live a fool the rest
>   Of his dull life."

But jests of this sort never seem so funny, after the first surprise has been felt. The best humor, like good wine, improves with age, and with each subsequent reading enjoyment grows. "Rudder Grange" bears this test; it is as fresh and charming now as when it was first written, and a new reading after it has been half forgotten will be even more relishful than the first.

Not even this book, well deserved as was its success, gave Mr. Stockton so wide a fame as one of his short stories, "The Lady or the Lady or the Tiger?" The artful way in which he Tiger? led his readers up to the crucial problem and then betrayed their confidence by refusing to solve it, cloaking this refusal under a pretext of inability to decide the question he had raised, was a stroke of humor that showed genius. It also showed commercial shrewdness, and had its reward. Curiosity was piqued, discussion was provoked, and debate on the merits of the question became quite a social "fad." When one thinks on what a slender basis literary fame is sometimes built, how fortuitous the gaining of it generally is, how frequently the public admires an author for that which is not best and most characteristic in his work, the stir that followed the publication of this story becomes more humorous than anything in the story itself. Since that time there has been not only a ready market, but an eager public, for whatever Mr. Stockton might write. He has not been tempted, however,

to over-production.   He has never shaken from the
tree the unripe fruits of his imagination merely
because they would sell, but has left them to grow
and ripen and mellow.

II.

As no reader will have failed to infer, Mr.
Stockton is first of all a clever writer of short
stories.   Collections of his magazine
Short stories.
stories have been made at various times
since 1884: "The Lady or the Tiger?" "The
Christmas Wreck," "The Bee Man of Orn," "Amos
Kilbright," "The Clocks of Rondaine," and "The
Watchmaker's Wife," — each volume containing,
besides the title story, several other tales.   These
volumes show Mr. Stockton's peculiar powers at their
best, and they give him an unquestioned place in
the front rank of American story-writers.   It is
true that these tales of his violate certain conven-
tions of literary art.   They seldom have a plot;
they frequently have no dialogue, consisting wholly
or mainly of narrative or monologue; there is not
much description, and no apparent attempt at effect.
One would say that stories constructed on such a
plan could hardly fail to be tedious, however brief,
since they lack so many of the things that other
story-tellers rely upon for effects.   Mr. Stockton's
method is vindicated by its success, not by its *a
priori* reasonableness.   There is such a thing, no

doubt, as "good form" in every performance that demands skill; but, after all, the main point is to do the thing. David's smooth stones from the brook seemed a very ineffective weapon with which to encounter a giant, and every military authority of the age would have pronounced his attempt hope-less; but Goliath found, to his cost, that the shep-herd's sling was mightier than the warrior's sword and spear. The Western oarsmen who His method rowed by the light of nature, and never- vindicated by success. theless beat crews trained to row scientifically, explained that theirs was called the "git thar" stroke. Mr. Stockton's method of story-telling may be similarly defined; it succeeds with him, but in another's hands it would very likely be a failure.

It must not be inferred that these stories lack literary merit. The contrary is the fact, as a critical study of them discloses. Take Literary one of the purely narrative stories, for merits. example, like "A Tale of Negative Gravity." It is told with so much of positive gravity, in so matter-of-fact a style, that one almost swallows it whole, — almost, but not quite. Now let one analyze that story, try to imitate its simple style, and however practised he may be in the art of expression he will finish his experiment with a new respect for the author's purely literary gifts. From one point of view Mr. Stockton may almost be said to have no style. There is nothing, one means, in the mere turn of his sentences, in his method of expression, that can be seized upon as character-istic, and laid away in memory as a sort of trade-mark by which the author's other work may be tested, judged, and identified. It is very plain, simple, flowing English, this style of Stockton's, the sort of writing that appears to the inexperienced the easiest thing in the world to do — until they have tried. The art that conceals art, until it can pass for nature itself, — that, we are continually told, is the highest type, and the secret of that Mr. Stockton has somehow caught.

These tales stamp their author as one of the most original of American writers. Though his style lacks mannerism or distinctive flavor, it *Originality.* is not so with the substance of his work. That has plenty of flavor, flavor of a kind so pecu-liar that his work could never by any accident be mistaken for that of any other writer. It might be not the easiest of tasks to tell whether an anony-mous essay or story should be fathered upon Mr. Howells or Mr. Aldrich; but it requires no such nicety of literary taste to recognize a story of Mr. Stockton's. One who has sufficient accuracy of taste to distinguish between a slice of roast beef and a raw potato, so to speak, will know the savor of his work wherever it is met. Other writers may be as original, in the strict sense of that term, but few, if any, are so individual, so unmistakably themselves and nobody else.

III.

MOST writers of short stories sooner or later are tempted to try their wings in the longer flight of a novel. It seems to be just _{Very like} about an even chance whether they suc- ^{failures.} ceed or fail, so different are the conditions of the two classes of fiction. One dislikes to use the word failure in connection with any of Mr. Stockton's work, yet "The Late Mrs. Null" and "The Hundredth Man" fall very far short of the relative excellence of his tales. The plots are very ingenious, the mystery surrounding Mrs. Null until the very last being quite worthy of Wilkie Collins; the dialogue is bright and amusing; considerable power of characterization is shown in these novels, a thing almost wholly absent from the tales. Yet withal there is a lack of power, and while the books are clever *tours de force* they are not work of lasting worth.

Why this should be is something of a puzzle, since writers of far less originality and force than. Mr. Stockton have produced better novels. The ingenious reader may easily propose _{A puzzle.} to himself several explanations, of which the following may be the most satisfactory, since it seems to fit all the facts known to the public. Mr. Stockton's peculiar power is best described by the word "droll." He excels in that juxtaposition of incongruities that is the essence of humor. Only, in his case, the incongruity is commonly not of ideas but of acts and situations; the incongruity of ideas is not put into words, as is the wont of most humorists, but suggested to the reader, suggested often with great delicacy and subtlety. The production of this effect on the mind of the reader is one that cannot be prolonged beyond a certain point without wearying him. A joke that a friend takes fifteen minutes to tell us is not likely to have a very sharp point when the end finally comes, and a writer who spins out his drollery to three hundred pages will find it becoming a weariness to the flesh. The very thing that constitutes Mr. Stockton's power in a story that can be read in a half-hour constitutes his weakness in a novel.

There is one other excellence in his novels for which Mr. Stockton has not yet been given credit. He has succeeded, at least in his Mrs. Null, in giving his story plenty of "local color." *His local color.* He was at one time a resident of Virginia, and the negro dialect and character have seldom been represented with a more sympathetic accuracy than by him. He may not have penetrated so deeply into the very heart of the negro as Mr. Page in his "Marse Chan" and other companion stories, but he has made himself not a bad second to the acknowledged first in this field.

As might, perhaps, be expected, Mr. Stockton has succeeded better in novelettes. Here he is almost as much at home as in the brief tale. "The Casting Away of Mrs. Lecks and Mrs. Aleshine" and its sequel, "The Dusantes," reach pretty nearly, if not quite, the high-water mark of our author. The first named of these stories is one of the best illustrations possible of his peculiar gift. The motive of the tale is the simplest possible: it is to show how two good New England women, bred in a narrow round of duties, and wonted to a certain moral and social standard of action until it had become second nature, would continue to act after their kind in whatever unaccustomed and startling circumstances they might be placed. The humor of the story consists almost wholly in the incongruity between the incidents of a shipwreck, involving a stay on a desert island, and the ingrained notions and habits of these women. This theme is treated with so much ingenuity, and with a touch so deft as to make of the story one of the most humorous things in literature. A little knowledge of New England village life is necessary to its fullest appreciation, but the reader is to be pitied whose imagination is not tickled by many of the scenes and incidents of this adventure.

Novelettes

One notes, in reading this story, what he cannot have failed to observe elsewhere, that the author has caught the trick of lifelike narration. The tale, in its sober, matter-of-fact style and its verisimilitude, might have been the work of Defoe or Hale. Neither of these writers is destitute of humor, especially Dr. Hale, but neither of them could have supplied the element in Stockton's stories that is their chief charm. The three are alike only in their faculty of telling a story so as to give it, while one is reading at least, all the semblance of the truth itself.

IV.

THE young folks know a good story-teller by instinct, and Mr. Stockton has from the first been His "juve-
niles." a prime favorite with them. As we have seen, his first book was composed of stories for children, and he has gone on writing for his youthful readers until his "juveniles" make quite a row, seven or more volumes. The best of these stories show a gift very similar to that which wins the favor of older readers, though it is rather a fantastic imagination than pure humor that inspires the best of them. Children, as a rule, have a quite rudimentary sense of humor, yet they are not incapable of appreciating droll things. They perceive most easily, however, that sort of humor which builders embody in gargoyles and other similar ornamentations, — grotesque distortions of types with which they are familiar in every-day life. Some of Mr. Stockton's fairy tales show a fertility of imagination that surpasses anything he has done in his other writings, and their whimsical absurdities are so gravely set forth that many a staid father while reading them to his children has been half inclined to accept them as veritable histories. It is noteworthy that in these stories the narrow line separating the fanciful from the burlesque is never crossed. Nobody could suspect from the writer's manner that he does not himself firmly believe in the reality of his marvellous creations. A false note here would be fatal, and none would be quicker to detect it than the readers of "St. Nicholas," where most of these tales have first appeared.

One of these books is of a more conventional sort, "A Jolly Fellowship." It is a very good story, only — and this is the worst one could say of it — a dozen other men might have written it as well as Mr. Stockton. It so completely lacks his distinctive qualities that, despite its general brightness, it must be ranked among his few failures; or, if that seem too harsh a word, his partial successes.

Mr. Stockton gives no signs of having exhausted his vein. He has made for himself a place unique and unapproachable in the regard of those who love good literature. Original to the verge of eccentricity, he provokes no comparisons with any writer. Nobody has ever thought of calling him "The American somebody or other," — a title bestowed on his fellow craftsmen, doubtless with an intent to compliment, though it is really the direst insult that can be offered to a man of letters, since it accuses him of being the weak echo of some European celebrity. No, the author of "Rudder Grange" is not "The American Lamb" nor the American anybody else, he is just Frank R. Stockton.

XIX.

JOAQUIN MILLER.

OF a poet, as well as of a prophet, it is sometimes true that he is not without honor save
in his own country and among his own people.
Something very like this might once have been said,
perhaps might be said even now, of Joaquin Miller.
There have been American men of letters before our
day, and there are others in our day, whom our kin
across the sea rate higher than we are accustomed
to rate them in America. In no other case easily re-
called has an American author's fame in his own land
been little more than the pale reflection His vogue in
of his transatlantic glory. Twenty years England.
ago Joaquin Miller was the lion of British society;
he was fêted and caressed by the rich and titled; he
was praised by the chorus of irresponsible, indolent
reviewers; his books ran through numerous editions
in two continents, — surely this was fame. The last
mark of condescending admiration was bestowed
upon him by his English admirers when one called
him "The American Byron." The epithet was not
wholly undeserved, for there were in his writings, as

Landor said of Byron, " things as strong as poison and
as original as sin." The British public has, of course,
long since recovered from its Miller " craze; " the
critics no longer say that he is the most original
and probably the greatest of our American poets;
and there are few living authors who are now more
utterly forgotten. Not long ago one who had occasion to purchase his collected poems, searched New
York high and low, but not a copy, new or second-
hand, could he find on sale. Of what other American
poet, living or dead, could this be true? The sober
critic hardly knows which phenomenon is the more
surprising and inexplicable, the suddenness of Mr.
Miller's undeserved fame, or the completeness of his
equally undeserved oblivion.

I.

CINCINNATUS HINER MILLER — or is it Heine, as
sometimes written? the authorities differ — was born
in the Wabash district of Indiana, November 10, 1841.
His parents moved to Oregon in 1854, and he was
brought up amid the rough, wild pioneer life of the
new territory, — surroundings well fitted to nourish
a poetic imagination, but affording few opportunities
of culture. His education was picked up anyhow or
nohow, — mostly the latter, one fancies, for
Education.
schools and books were scarce in Oregon
in those days. Long before he reached manhood
young Miller seems to have been thrown on his own

resources, and to have made trial of more than one means of livelihood. He had the inevitable experience in mining, and succeeded in it no better than Bret Harte; he studied law for a time; he was an express messenger in Idaho, — which meant rough work, small pay, and the daily risk of life, in those days; he was editor of a paper. This was "seeing life" on a pretty generous scale and in a less harmful way than is affected by the more or less gilded youth of our cities.

The journalistic experience to which allusion has been made was very brief. Mr. Miller became editor of the " Democratic Register," of Eugene, Oregon, in 1863, but the paper was soon after suppressed by military authority, the editor having been guilty of what were deemed disloyal utterances. From what can be learned, the paper seems to have been a "copperhead" sheet, following the lead of such men as Vallandigham, and it doubtless deserved its fate. When we recall, however, Journalist. that the editor was but twenty-two years of age, and that this was his first venture in politics, — his last, too, it would seem, — we shall not pass a harsh sentence of condemnation on him. After this conspicuous failure, Mr. Miller won something very like success. He opened a law office in Cañon City, and soon gained a fair practice. It was here that one of the most exciting adventures of his career befell him. According to the story, Cañon City was invested by hostile Indians, and Miller led an expedition

against them into their own country; but after a
long and bloody campaign, he was finally beaten
back, leaving his dead on the field. As this episode
is related by the veracious G. Washington Moon,
Hon. F. R. S. L., one cannot doubt its literal accuracy. Not long after, the young lawyer and Indian-
fighter was made judge of the Grant County court,
Lawyer and   which office he held from 1866 to 1870.
judge.   Had he continued in the way he thus
began, he might have carved out for himself a
notable career as jurist and public servant. Men
of far less native endowment and force of character
have been governors and senators from the new
States of the West. But his weird was upon him,
as the Scotch say; he was doomed to the pains and
penalties, as well as born to the joys, of authorship.

II.

MR. MILLER began to write in boyhood, ignorant
of the rules of versification and even of English
grammar. He wrote because he was irresistibly
impelled, and with the least possible encouragement
from without; for, though he first published a collection of his verses in paper covers,
First writings.   modestly calling them " Specimens," and
later a volume with the title " Joaquin et al.," it does
not appear that he gained more than a local fame as
a poet, and not too much even of that. It was hardly
to be expected that poetry would find a ready market

in a new country where every energy was absorbed in the struggle to wring from nature a mere subsistence.

For many years he diligently availed himself of such means of culture as came within his reach, reading with equal pleasure and profit authors ancient and modern as they came to hand (the former necessarily in translations), and practising his art in secret. He cherished the conviction that he was born to be a poet, and could he but break his birth's invidious bar and grasp the skirts of happy chance, fame and fortune would be his. It was his desire to visit England, where, for some reason, he believed that he would meet with more encouragement than at home. The event justified his prescience. _{Visits England.}

In 1870 he realized his long-cherished desire, and the following year saw the publication in London of his "Songs of the Sierras." The same year the book also appeared in Boston, with the imprint of Roberts Brothers. The name Joaquin, which appeared on the titlepage, and by which only the poet was known for some years, was _{Songs of the Sierras.} a reminiscence of his legal experience. It had once fallen to his lot to defend a Mexican brigand named Joaquin Murietta, and he substituted his client's Christian name for his own, in the belief, doubtless, that it better suited the character of his verse.

It was the publication of this volume that caused the *furore* in England that has already been described. This was really one of the great literary successes of our generation, so far as immediate and wide popularity and social honors measure success. To be sure, it was founded on British insularity and British ignorance. The English critic, and to some degree the English public also, is always on the watch for something original in American literature, something distinctively national, something racy of the soil. He has an ingrained conviction that our literature is, for the most part, a weak echo of his country's, and that few of our authors are truly American. But he fails to distinguish between what is original and what is merely *bizarre*, and individual affectation frequently imposes itself on him as the true flavor of American life.

The British admiration of Joaquin Miller was, therefore, based on an entirely erroneous idea of the literary significance of his writings. Except in his themes, few of our American poets have been less American. His stories, — for most of his poems are rhymed and versified tales of adventure, — as to their details, have the true wild Western savor, but in all other respects his work is purely British. It has already been intimated that the British critic did well to describe him as " The American Byron." That form of description, as has been remarked heretofore, is generally an insult that vainly tries to disguise itself as a compliment. In this case the phrase escapes being insulting by being accurately descriptive. Joaquin Miller is the American Byron — just that, and only that — in his " Songs of the Sierras." His heroes are Byron's characters masquerading in California costumes; Walker is a Lara in sombrero and serape, and Kit Carson is Don Juan in the garb of scout and Indian fighter. Byron's influence can be traced in every poem and almost in every line. One is not, perhaps, justified in saying that Joaquin Miller would never have written these songs if he had not soaked his mind in Byron, but he would certainly have written them far differently in that case.

III.

ONE thing should have saved the British critic from this mistake of his, — the lack of artistic merit in this first book of Mr. Miller's. Whatever merits it may be allowed to contain, the merit of good workmanship is certainly absent. The instructed reader should have perceived at once that if here was a poet born, here was not a poet made. The critic might have perceived also, what is certainly there, — evidence that this was a poet who had an innate faculty of expression, that might be improved by practice and polished by the learning and following of rules, but not without attractiveness in its natural wildness.

What is bad in this book is bad without disguise, so fatuously bad that one never ceases wondering how an author capable of such stuff could ever do anything good. Yet the good, in turn, Extremes meet.
is so strong and so beautiful as to make the reader

temporarily insensible to irregularities and inequalities of style, as well as to gross defects of taste. That this is no exaggeration let the following lines testify: —

> " I lay in my hammock: the air was heavy
> And hot and threatening; the very heaven
> Was holding its breath; the bees in a bevy
> Hid under my thatch; and birds were driven
> In clouds to the rocks in a hurried whirr
> As I peer'd down by the path for her.
> She stood like a bronze bent over the river,
> The proud eyes fix'd, the passion unspoken —
> When the heavens broke like a great dyke broken.
> Then, ere I fairly had time to give her
> A shout of warning, a rushing of wind
> And the rolling of clouds and a deafening din
> And a darkness that had been black to the blind
> Came down, as I shouted, ' Come in! come in!
> Come under the roof, come up from the river,
> As up from a grave — come now, or come never! '·
> The tassel'd tops of the pines were as weeds,
> The red-woods rock'd like to lake-side reeds,
> And the world seem'd darken'd and drown'd for ever."

That is almost incomparably good, — not quite perfect in workmanship, but so full of passion and fire as to atone for any defects in form. When one reads that, and some other things in this volume, one can almost pardon the British critic who wrote, fresh from the reading of it: " Of all American poetry in recent years, that of Mr. Joaquin Miller is the freshest. He **A British** is a new poet in the proper sense of the **criticism.** term. He owes allegiance to no transatlantic masters, and he is no servile imitator of the modern minstrelsy of our own country. In outward

form — in the mechanism of his poetry — he of course
follows the fashion of the times; but the spirit is new,
the tone is individual and distinct. In his poems for
the first time the prairies, the Sierras, and the new
and old life of the Far West of America, have been
fairly poetized, so to speak." One can almost pardon
this, but not quite; for it is the duty of the critic not
to let himself be carried off his feet by his emotions,
and to maintain his coolness of judgment when his
admiration is most stirred. The trouble with this
critic was that he admired not wisely but too well,
and that, approaching his author with a preconceived
theory of American poetry, he misjudged the facts
before him. So absurd, however, did the whole tribe
of British critics become, that on the publication of
Mr. Miller's second volume, "Songs of the Sun-
Lands," we find the "Westminster Review" soberly
exhorting the poet after this fashion: "Mr. Miller
must be careful that he does not buy ele- More of the
gance at too dear a price. We ourselves same sort.
prefer the roughness of the backwoods of America to
all the drawing-room conventionalities of Europe.
We prefer Mr. Joaquin Miller's native reed-pipe to
any guitar." Now it is about an even chance whether
Mr. Miller's "native reed-pipe" (a pretty phrase, is
it not?) sends forth music or discord, and this exhor-
tation not to be too fine, not to condescend too much
to the polish of civilization, was, had the critic but
known it, the worst advice he could have given to the
poet, — not to mention that it was wholly wasted, for

Joaquin Miller's besetting sin has never been too much regard for the conventional.

In truth, this second volume showed a marked advance in the poetic art. It showed that the poet was gradually acquiring some knowledge of versification, though it also warranted a prediction that he would never become complete master of conventional forms of expression. There is, and to the last there will be something untamed and untutored about his verse; it is as lawless as the outlaws whom it so often celebrates, but, like them, often unexpectedly reveals elemental traits of strength and beauty. And yet this general characterization of his work is hardly fair; sweeping statements are seldom quite fair, until they are so qualified with exceptions that the original text is scarcely discernible. Here and there one finds, even in his first volume, a choice bit that could hardly be made more perfect by the most painstaking workmanship. Here is an instance: —

Choice bits.

> " Life knows no dead so beautiful
>   As is the white cold coffin'd past;
> This I may love nor be betray'd:
>   The dead are faithful to the last.
> I am not spouseless — I have wed
> A memory — a life that 's dead."

One can hardly say that in his later volumes these bits occur more frequently, but they do occur, — witness these stanzas, prefixed to "The Rhyme of the Great River," in "Songs of the Mexican Seas" (1887): —

" Rhyme on, rhyme on in reedy flow,
   O river, rhymer ever sweet!
   The story of thy land is meet,
The stars stand listening to know.

" Rhyme on, O river of the earth!
   Gray father of the dreadful seas,
   Rhyme on! the world upon its knees
Shall yet invoke thy wealth and worth.

" Rhyme on, the reed is at thy mouth,
   O kingly minstrel, mighty stream!
   Thy Crescent City, like a dream,
Hangs in the heaven of my South.

" Rhyme on, rhyme on! these broken strings
   Sing sweetest in this warm south wind;
   I sit thy willow banks and bind
A broken harp that fitful sings."

As may be inferred from even the brief extracts given above, Mr. Miller is at his best in his lyrics. His longer narrative poems are weak and confused in structure, though they often contain some of his strongest passages. His blank, unrhymed verse, the severest test of a poet, could not well be of poorer quality; it is verbose, spasmodic, bombastic. Qualification must again be made to these general statements. One of his longer poems, in his " Songs of the Sun-Lands," " The Isles of the Amazons," must be rated as, on the whole, the finest specimen of his work. Into it he has put all his strength, and, as he seems temporarily to have forgotten his affectations and mannerisms, his lines glow

The Isles of the Amazons.

with tropical passion, and thrill the reader with the vividness and originality of their imagery and their spontaneous vigor of expression. The lack of proportion, the sins against good taste, the rawness and crudeness of sentiment that so repel the reader in some of his work, are inconspicuous here. Extracts would do no justice to this noble poem, which must be read and admired as a whole.

In the dedication of one of his latest volumes, Mr. Miller asks, somewhat plaintively: "And may I not ask in return, now at the last, when the shadows begin to grow long, something of that consideration which, thus far, has been accorded almost entirely by strangers?" If by "consideration" the poet means that fulsome and foolish praise that the English chorussed twenty years ago, his hope is vain. He Lacks critical probably took it seriously when the sapient faculty. London critics assured him that he was a greater, because a more original, poet than Lowell or Bryant. We may safely infer from his writings that he has little faculty of self-criticism, — that all his work appears to him of nearly equal worth, and that he is unconscious of his many and flagrant faults. This alone can account for his lawless trampling on the conventionalities of the poet's art. The fame that he would claim as his right will never be awarded him by the readers of the present day, whatever the readers of the future may say. But Mr. Miller has, nevertheless, just cause of complaint against his countrymen.

There has been a natural resentment of the unwise puffery of the London press, and in consequence the poet has never received his true meed of praise. Certain personal eccentricities have also stood between him and a just appreciation of his work. There is so much that is finely imaginative in his verse, so much that is genuine in feeling and powerful in expression, that, in spite of his maddening shortcomings, the perverse wilfulness of his errors, he deserves and should before this have been awarded by general suffrage, an honored place well up on the roll of American poets.

INDEX.

INDEX.